Praise for ***Way of the Junglepreneur*** and the Author

Way of the Junglepreneur contains absolutely amazing business concepts and frameworks which are required for every business person currently in challenging and dynamic business environments. The approaches work in all emerging markets and David Fasanya has written a business book that will inspire generations of business people for many years to come

—**Alex C.C. Pun**, Regional Product Manager,
Phillips. Shanghai, China.

Way of the Junglepreneur is one book on challenging business environments I'd have if I could have just one. It contains powerful, practical and solid advice on how to overcome business challenges with confidence. David has done a great job on this one and it is a must-read for anyone who wants to get on in business globally.

—**Adedoja Allen (Mrs)**, MD/CEO, City 105.1FM. Lagos, Nigeria.
Winner of Best Radio Station in Lagos, 2014.

Way of the Junglepreneur is a very well written and contemporary business book which deserves my highest commendation to David. Anyone who's ever wanted to run a successful business or is currently running a business and wants to know how succeed and survive in a challenging business environment can confidently benefit from the down-to-earth knowledge in this book.

—**Patrick Dwamena**, CEO, J&Q Industries Limited, Ghana,
Producers of Ecospa Mineral Water.
(Ecospa is the preferred water brand in Ghana).

WAY
of the
Junglepreneur

WAY of the Junglepreneur

Art of Succeeding and Surviving in Tough Business Terrains

DAVID OLUDOTUN FASANYA

For permission requests, please address
Cedar Forge Press
7300 West Joy Road
Dexter, Michigan 48130

Published 2014 by Cedar Forge Press
Printed in the United States of America

18 17 16 15 14 1 2 3 4 5

ISBN 978-1-936672-90-5

Library of Congress Control Number: 2014945009

I dedicate this book to the almighty God,
my wonderful family and friends.

Note to Readers

This publication contains the opinions, ideas and philosophy of the author. It is intended to educate and provide helpful and informative material on the subjects addressed. Since each factual situation is different, the suggestions, frameworks and strategies outlined in this book may not be suitable for every individual. They are therefore not guaranteed or warranted to produce any particular results. This book is sold with the understanding that the information is not intended to render legal, financial, accounting or other professional advice or services to the reader. Before adopting any of the suggestions in this book or drawing inferences from this book the reader should consult his or her own advisor concerning that individual's specific circumstances.

The author has taken precautions in the preparation of this book and believes that the facts presented in the book are accurate as of the date it was written, but no warranty is made with respect to the accuracy or completeness of the information or references contained herein, and neither the author, nor the publisher assumes any fault for any errors or omissions. Both the author and the publisher specifically disclaim any responsibility for any liability, loss, risk, personal or otherwise, which is incurred as a consequence, directly or indirectly, of the use and application of any of the contents of this book.

Contents

Introduction
The Junglepreneur Philosophy

Imagine being a businessperson in a challenging environment, making so much effort but barely scratching the surface. Imagine the feelings of exasperation you get when, despite all your efforts, it appears that the tough terrain around you is unyielding. Yet you know that the terrain has a lot of potential, and you have it in you to succeed. Now take a peek into your glorious future and imagine that finally you have gained the knowledge, information, skills, tools, and experience needed to tame these terrains. Imagine the pride and joy that your loved ones have about your success. Imagine your personal satisfaction now that your dreams are coming true and you are getting to live the life you have always desired. What I have just recounted is the possible journey of a businessperson in a tough terrain. Different people are at different points in this journey, but perhaps you can relate to some of the challenges and triumphs I have described. Well, so can I. My name is David Oludotun Fasanya, and I am a Junglepreneur. You can be one too.

I want to share with you a roadmap for achieving your dreams and thriving in any business terrain. The roadmap is the concept of Junglepreneurship, which teaches you how to tackle any business environment, overcome challenges, maximize opportunities, and use them to succeed. It is an exciting roadmap for how you can become the ultimate tough-terrain businessperson, a Junglepreneur—or become a better Junglepreneur. I add that last statement because, from my interactions so far with many people all over the world on this concept, I have realized that Junglepreneurship is real and has been waiting in the wings to be revealed for a long time. Up to this point it had been lost among the other definitions of businesspeople. Now the message has been discovered, and it boldly stands out in its own right as an art and a philosophy. Junglepreneurship has come of age and is becoming a growing movement of people in different tough terrains from all over the world. In this new turbulent business age, it is finally the time of the Junglepreneurs. What you are about to read is the synthesis and message of the invaluable philosophy of Junglepreneurship and a guide to being a Junglepreneur. The message is out there now, and I am just the messenger.

Why did I write about such odd-sounding concepts as Junglepreneurship and the Junglepreneur? The seeds were probably sown many years ago. However, only recently did I decide to finally write this book while on a visit to the city of Accra in Ghana. On this occasion I had flown from the UK to West Africa for business and charity purposes. I had been financially supporting a charitable endeavor started by a Ghana-born British doctor and her friends from Liverpool. These wonderful and talented doctors had identified high childbirth mortality rates for women in some remote parts of Ghana and wanted to reduce them. They found the cause to be a lack of proper training for the local midwives, who were the predominant medical caregivers for many pregnant women. The doctors would visit Ghana from the UK a few times in the year with their practical equipment to train midwives in safe and modern childbirth delivery methods. Through these workshops, they have significantly reduced childbirth mortality rates.

On this trip I had been invited to come and see for myself the work they were doing in the field. My 4x4 vehicle left from Accra to visit a village on the outskirts of the city. The traffic on the highway leading out of the city was heavy and slow-moving. Our surrounding atmosphere was thick with vehicle exhaust fumes and suffused intermittently with the sounds of honking horns being used as a form of expression by the exasperated drivers. Suddenly I heard a male voice outside my window, yelling, “Buy your handset, sir!” The smiling, sweat-drenched, and dust-covered young man looked at me, quite pleased that he had finally caught my attention. He had been tapping at my car window, and I had not heard him because of the intriguing activity going on around me. I had been caught up in one of the famous West African traffic jams popularly called a *go-slow*, in which hawkers often spring out of nowhere to sell all manner of items. It has developed over the years into a phenomenon of mobile supermarkets in traffic. Like a mushroom, the go-slow market can suddenly appear anywhere the daily snarl of traffic jams occurs. In this traffic go-slow supermarket, different items are sold by hawkers who use their arms and neck as shop hangers to display various items. They do this while dashing at amazing speed between vehicles to make quick sales, at the same time keeping watch for law enforcement agents bent on eradicating street trading. This particular hawker was trying to sell me a mobile phone handset right there on the highway. My mind then flickered through other shopping scenes I had seen on the High Street shops of Europe, in the gold souk markets of Dubai, and in the vast underground shopping malls of Montreal. There were undeniable similarities. Though these other places had much slicker salespeople in fine shops, by and large the dusty hawker in traffic and the slick salespeople elsewhere were all just trying to get by.

I then reflected on my own varied business experiences in the different parts of the world over the last two decades, as well as those of many other people I knew closely. The realization hit me that, though business as a jungle was a familiar concept, business all over the world was really and truly junglelike in many respects. What struck me was that the business world actually held realities that could be considered from another perspective. From this viewpoint, I saw that the business world has different ecosystems all working together. One could liken parts of a business ecosystem to a tough, junglelike terrain, filled with its own food, resources, prey, predators, challenges, trials, and triumphs. In this tough business ecosystem, a certain breed sits at the top of the food chain and can survive and even thrive in this junglelike setting. With this outlook, there were enough reasons for me to make broad arguments about the perspective of Junglepreneurship solely from epistemological or ontological positions. However, I was rather consumed at this time by the burning desire to write, a practical, down-to-earth book about the business jungle and the laws that guide it. So this book tries to capture the unwritten rules of the game of business survival by the person at the top of the food chain—the Junglepreneur.

About Tough Terrains, the New Law of Survival, and Junglepreneurship

Today's world can be generally challenging with its ever-present uncertainties, turmoil, shocks, and risks, which have made business terrains very tough. On the other hand, the modern-day business world has also produced some of the greatest business opportunities ever known to mankind. One of these opportunities is the Bali Pact of December 2013, in which 159 member nations of the World Trade Organization agreed to remove tariffs and regulations that were obstacles to global trade. However, the challenges and opportunities in business seem to have both been shaped by the efficacy and application of one particular law, which has also weathered all storms and seems to have held sway no matter the conditions. This is an old law generally derived from the theories of evolution and natural selection, which were later socially interpreted to depict high levels of competition in business. This is the law that ascribed success and survival to the fittest: the universal law of survival. If I were to give a more primal description, it could be termed here as "those sets of actions and inactions that creative beings will display so as to ensure the safety of their continued means, the provision of their immediate sustenance, and the certainty of their posterity."

However, though the old law of survival still has its place, in light of modern times, I argue that there has been an evolution from the old law of survival into a new one. The new law of survival says that the most capable beings will thrive and survive economically and otherwise. I will soon explain what capable means under this new law, which will be exceedingly challenging and also rewarding to live by. However, the new law of survival can be argued here to be what will drive and motivate a significant amount of human activity—economic and otherwise—for years to come. So based on these, the concept of Junglepreneurship can be defined as "the survival-driven process of creatively maximizing all opportunities to resourcefully commence a business endeavor, overcome challenges, and thrive in the endeavor by using all legal means necessary." So the Junglepreneur can then be defined as "the person who can build a business in any location and then ensure that it survives and thrives by all legal means, through always being Creative, Adaptable, Persistent, Aware, Brave, Linked, and Energized." Thus, the Junglepreneur is CAPABLE, and that capability is part of the definition of the new law of survival. Jungle CAPABLE means the Junglepreneur has the ability to actually tame any tough business jungle and to survive and thrive in it. How the Junglepreneur does this will become clear as you read this book.

How is the Junglepreneur Different?

In modern tough, junglelike business terrains, the new law of survival is king, and the Junglepreneur by reason of composition and training is the most attuned person to its rules. Therefore the Junglepreneur is fundamentally different from other businesspeople. The key distinctions of the Junglepreneur are his or her unique formation process, the location of his or her business activity, and then his or her immense survival capacity in the face of rapidly changing environments. The distinctions that make the Junglepreneur unique will be elaborated upon further in the first chapter of this book. The new law of survival knows no geographical boundaries, but it is applicable in all terrains to the junglelike business setting I have just mentioned. The reality is that business everywhere is mostly about survival and dependent on who controls resources. Despite the brutally competitive nature of business, the other option is to try to succeed in a creative way by using the necessary skills, practical tactics, and tools required to thrive. Whichever choice one makes, in many cases it is the rules of the game that are contained in the new law of survival that eventually determine success.

The Junglepreneur Philosophy

This book is about how to thrive. It is about a different way of capturing the manner in which business really plays out in practice. Since modern-day business can be said to be unconventional by its very nature, it requires people with unconventional means to succeed and survive in it. The way of the Junglepreneur is unique, practical, demanding, versatile, and unconventional, but it is also completely ethical and legal. The way of the Junglepreneur is not a one-size-fits-all solution, but the philosophy postulates innovative ways of thinking and going about business. It also advocates a different way of acting in order to succeed and survive in the business jungle as it is today. The philosophy of the Junglepreneur is different but simple, and the Junglepreneur's way of life is unconventionally based on the new law of survival.

How to Use This Book

This book looks at the Junglepreneur from a business perspective, but it is not limited to business only. The philosophy undergirding these principles may be useful in many other areas of life. The book closely considers some of the challenges, triumphs, and experiences that may be encountered in the complexity of unusual business ecosystems. This way it should serve as a useful resource that can be used to attain success in any tough business environment. The information in this book is synthesized based on practical, hands-on experience in the business jungle in both the developing and developed world, including interactions with and studies made of numerous successful businesspeople all around the globe. So this book is useful as an insight for people who are just starting out in business or for emerging businesspeople who have already had a taste of the tough business world and need all the extra help, encouragement, and tips they can get. For the already established and successful person, it will give refreshing perspectives on business and life concepts. It may even stimulate a complete redefinition of who you are as a businessperson.

Simply said, there is likely to be something here for everyone, at every level of success. The book format has a simple arrangement of chapters with clear topical outlines of what each chapter contains. The content in the chapters is interwoven with stories, quotes, anecdotes, and scenarios that are used to explain particular points. It is recommended that the whole book be read to fully grasp the essence of the information in it. This can be done by reading the chapters sequentially or in any order, according to the topics you are interested in. However, to get a good foundation, it is suggested that Chapters 1 and 2 be read first because this is where you will find more details about the concept of Junglepreneurship, the Junglepreneur, and tough business terrains. From Chapter 3 to Chapter 9 the book delves into real specifics on how you can become a Junglepreneur or be a better one. Here, specialized concepts, tools, business cases, and frameworks are shared with you that have been specifically synthesized for this purpose. The book then concludes with Chapter 10 on the important topic of the Junglepreneur's Attitude. For readers who still require more information or clarification about some subjects, there is a bibliography and notes section at the end of the book, which adds further detail and context. If just you alone can learn from this book and achieve successful results in any challenging business location, then all the effort put into writing this book will be worthwhile. Enjoy.

David Oludotun Fasanya
December, 2014.

One
Who is the Junglepreneur?

The will to win, the desire to succeed, the urge to reach your full potential … these are the keys that will unlock the door to personal excellence.
—Confucius

Business is a combination of war and sport.
—Andre Maurois, biographer of Benjamin Disraeli

I start with my story and how the seeds for the Junglepreneur were sown many years ago. As a sixteen-year-old in the late '80s, I found myself in blue overalls, working in a factory. It was my time off from school during the holidays, and instead of all the fun things a teenager on holiday could do, I was working unhappily on an assembly line. My time in the factory was to continue during most holidays and breaks for some years. During this time, though, I learned early the qualities of hard work, perseverance, and humility. I was able to mingle with people at all levels of life, even though I was actually from a comfortable background and the factory belonged to my father. My father, a businessman who had set up the mid-sized factory to manufacture consumer products, believed that despite my comfortable upbringing I needed to learn the virtues of hard work early in my formative years.

So while my friends had the luxury of playing during the holiday break, my dad sent me to his factory and offered no preferential treatment. Under a tough foreman, I did the exact same work that all the other workers did, and I learned the ropes the hard way. After some time, I was able to roll a 200-kilo drum or operate any machine just as well as my blue-collared coworkers, and I earned their respect. My factory experiences also exposed me to various other business issues relating to staff welfare, material sourcing, regulatory compliance, warehousing, and distribution, among others. From these experiences, I first learned what it was like for a business to operate in truly tough terrains.

My father was previously a major importer and distributor of chemicals, building materials, power tools, sanitary wares, and commodities, which he had traded in very large volumes in Nigeria. However, the country faced political and economic challenges in the '80s, which made it difficult for businessmen to get import licenses, and to survive he decided to diversify from trading into manufacturing. Though he had trained as a cost and management accountant, he purposely set out to build a good team made up of people with other diverse qualifications and skills to help him realize his goal. He subsequently opened a factory for manufacturing consumer products and industrial chemicals. Furthermore, so that he could be in better control of his business without relying on import licenses, he developed import substitution-based production formulas, which could work using at least 80 percent locally sourced raw-material inputs. He succeeded fairly well in this venture and eventually pioneered products that achieved 100 percent locally sourced inputs.

My father had trained in England for many years and worked all over the world, so he realized that we were in a very tough terrain if ever there was one. He wanted me to learn as much as possible very early in life about how to survive and thrive. Later on, after graduating from university, I still played a role in the factory but soon went off to cut my own teeth in different areas of business, which I conducted for many years in developing countries in Africa before relocating to Europe. My time on that continent then taught me about what it also takes to do business in developed regions around the world. Even though I have been living in the UK for a while now, I was born in Zambia and later moved to Nigeria. Adding my factory experiences during my formative years, I have garnered in total about 22 years of cumulative business experience, out of which about 19 years can be attributed to direct business experience in both developing and developed countries. In my own business journey, I have encountered a fair share of challenges and struggles along the way in various tough business terrains, and I am fortunate enough to have found ways to overcome them with reasonable success.

As part of my journey, I have been a prolific businessperson and at various times have managed, founded, or been involved with numerous companies at various levels. For instance, I co-founded and managed an IT security and biometrics company in Nigeria about 15 years ago. For this company, suppliers and service providers had been sourced mainly from France, Switzerland, and Canada with the intention of deploying the cutting-edge solutions into the market. This was a new area in this market at that time, so managing the venture and trying to succeed in it was a real struggle. However, despite the trials, within five years I had led the company into achieving seven-figure sales turnovers and had successfully delivered many large projects.

In another company I led at the executive level, we were the last entrant in a developed manufacturing-servicing market in Africa, and the odds were really stacked against our success. The business provided manufacturing-support machines, components, parts, and after-sales service to manufacturers. In this case I was able to establish direct relationships with original equipment manufacturers based in America, and I negotiated huge supply discounts, which helped to gain reasonable market share. We eventually built up a direct customer base of over 60 mid-sized manufacturing companies with good sales turnovers.

In the UK I also co-founded an online retail service, which sought to bridge the gap between retailers in Europe and customers in emerging markets in Africa. This service achieved thousands of successful transactions and has now evolved into a full trading and e-commerce portal. It presently provides e-commerce-enabled online stores, integrated payment gateway services, trade consulting, management information, and affiliate programs.

Looking back on my own journey, I realized that my own experience might offer a roadmap for those looking to tread in difficult business terrains. I also spoke to several much more successful people than myself, who had experienced some of the same hardships on their way to prosperity and could give battle-tested information on what worked and didn't work in tough terrains. This book was thus inspired by my own scars as well as those of very many people doing business in difficult terrains. Much of what you will read here comes from what I have personally experienced or learned. Other examples come from my direct interactions with other people who have also experienced tough terrains. Some of the content also comes from studies of different achievers from all over the world who have encountered junglelike terrains in one form or another. These people have given something back to the world in the form of a quote, comment, or detailed experience, which has been useful in writing this book.

Despite the difficulty, writing this book proved to be a rewarding experience. In my peculiar situation, I consider myself very lucky to have encountered so many challenging circumstances in business and in life, which were well beyond my years, and succeeded. To have also had access to many other people who have passed through hard terrains and made it is an extra bonus. So based on all these, what you will read in this book are the forms of advice, teachings, and words spoken in the ears of the person who is operating in a tough, junglelike business terrain. I call that person the Junglepreneur.

The Future of Business

The concept of the Junglepreneur involves considering business terrains as they exist all over the world. So before delving fully into the notion of the Junglepreneur, it is important at this stage to first consider where the business world is at present, how global business issues work now, the implications of these, and what is likely to be the evolution of global business in the coming future. After the financial crisis of 2008, business affairs as we know it have changed dramatically—possibly for a long time to come. During that time, I wrote an international business research paper about the effects of the subprime mortgage crisis on financial institutions.[1] In the course of writing the paper, interviews were conducted with different experts and stakeholders in different continents who had direct engagement with the unfolding global phenomenon. My findings were astonishing: the research discovered that the crisis had actually spread to almost all the international financial markets. As of May 2008, the sum of $323 billion had been lost in asset write-downs by the top 100 biggest banks and securities firms in the world, and apparently that was just the tip of the iceberg, as the world would later discover.[2]

Due to a classic case of herd behavior, as will be discussed later in this book, the institutions affected by the crisis were in every continent, in a kind of global financial contagion effect. This made real the fact that world markets had become really integrated and codependent. Moreover, there was an immense loss of confidence among global financial players. Furthermore, governments, regulatory authorities, risk-management institutions, and rating agencies appeared to have been caught off-guard by the unfolding events and seemed visibly amazed and embarrassed. These circumstances, and the rapid spread of the crisis internationally, in effect transformed most of the global business world into tough business terrains almost overnight.

No one took direct responsibility for the crisis, but it was clear from the results of my study and from so many studies by others that there would be far-reaching implications. These would include recessional effects on major economies, with the effects of the crisis lasting for a long time to come. With time this proved true, which could be seen later with the collapse of global financial giants, the recent Eurozone crises, and previously unimagined sovereign defaults in some government bonds. Furthermore, there have been some government bankruptcies and even governmental shutdowns due to large budget deficits, which were mainly inflated due to institutional bailouts and market interventions during the crisis.

My study recommended a complete overhaul of the then BASEL II (Basel Committee on Banking Supervision Second Accord) and that adjustments be made to include a hybrid merger of financial and operational risk-measurement approaches. It then also recommended the review of financial stress-testing procedures to accommodate possible future systemic crises, the strengthening of corporate governance mechanisms, and the adoption of a "stake-steward" corporate governance approach, which would achieve more inclusive responsibility among corporate players. The study was just one out of so many other reports that came out as a result of the crisis, but the important thing at that time was that every stakeholder contributed ideas to ensure that the effects of the 2008 financial crisis were mitigated.

Now, years removed from the crisis, even though there has been remarkable recovery in some economies, confidence is just gradually returning to the global markets, and the business terrain remains very sensitive and affected still. Moreover, a reasonable number of governments, markets, and institutions are still experiencing significant spill-over effects from the crisis. I continue to carry out research into contemporary international business issues and hold regular discussions with stakeholders. Based on all the foregoing, my view is that for many years to come, global business will be conducted in increasingly tougher environments with a continuous set of new rules, regulations, and players. However, on a brighter note, we can also look forward to developments such as these:[3]

- Increased sophistication in globalization trends and integration of international markets;
- Massive technological, communication, and transportation innovations;[4]
- Emergence of unusual forms of international corporations and management;
- Greater balance between economic needs and ecological responsibility;
- Evolution in the models of finance, securities, and transactional methods;[5]
- Redefinition of existing business theories;
- Increased power of the general society over the control of money;[6]
- Renewed emphasis on production-based economies;
- Advancements in global political and socioeconomic governance mechanisms;
- Increased tolerance and maximization of cultural diversities; and
- Newer business opportunities in multiple geographic terrains.

The Junglepreneur

This massive shift to come in global business will require businesspersons with the flexibility to adapt quickly to rapid changes. Furthermore, business leaders internationally have realized that one of the ways to achieve full global economic recovery is to encourage large numbers of new small and medium businesses to develop and to encourage new businesspeople to enter the market with innovations. So in the years ahead there will be a massive global drive to build more new businesses. Huge resources will continue to be provided for incubation centers, online presence, marketing, management training, and seed funding for business people.

However, a key missing ingredient, which will greatly complement all these initiatives, is a resource to prepare businesspeople for the tough business terrains they will face in the new business world. This is because it is all a different ball game now. Businesspeople will really need to see things from multiple perspectives to be able to tame different business environments. They will need the right mindset, philosophy, frameworks, paradigms, and tools to survive and thrive in the new rapidly evolving and turbulent terrain. Businesspeople who are able to do these will be at a great advantage in the new business setting. In my opinion, this missing ingredient is the concept of Junglepreneurship because tough terrains will be experienced in all parts of the world by different people. Part of the new mindset required will also be the application of the new law of survival. Based on my own interpretation, the new law of survival is not just about survival of the fittest, but it is also that the most capable will be the ones to survive and thrive. So in the present-day global economy and for the foreseeable future, I argue that Junglepreneurship and the new law of survival will play significant roles.

In the introduction of the book, I defined the Junglepreneur as "the person who can build a business in any location and then ensure that it survives and thrives by all legal means, through always being Creative, Adaptable, Persistent, Aware, Brave, Linked, and Energized"—by being Jungle CAPABLE.

Components of being Jungle CAPABLE start with creativity, and this means being able to use available resources to make something unique and different. Adaptability means being flexible with your environment. Persistence is remaining steadfast and persevering in the face of challenges. Awareness means knowing what is going on around you and being informed about the terrain. Being brave means remaining courageous in the face of fear or challenges. Linked means maintaining your network and interconnections within the terrain. Energetic means always generating, preserving, and deploying your energy mainly toward achieving your goal of succeeding in your terrain.

I also said the Junglepreneur is quite distinct as a businessperson, and with the clarification of being Jungle CAPABLE, this assertion may begin to get clearer. Nevertheless, commenting that the Junglepreneur is distinct could still seem curious in a world where all businesspeople tend to be categorized under a general umbrella. So to shed more light on this, let us now consider further those distinctions which make the Junglepreneur different.

Junglepreneur Distinctions

There are many distinctions that make the Junglepreneur unique. However, among many others, we will focus on the key distinctions of the Junglepreneur, the ones that are notable and earn the Junglepreneur immense respect and maybe even some awe. These key distinctions are:

1. Formation process of the Junglepreneur.
2. Capacity of the Junglepreneur to excel in rapidly changing environments.
3. Location of the Junglepreneur in very tough business terrains.

These three distinctions have been crystallized into what is called the Junglepreneur FOCAL Point, with *FO* representing *Formation*, *CA* representing *Capacity*, and *L* representing *Location*.

The Junglepreneur FOCAL Point

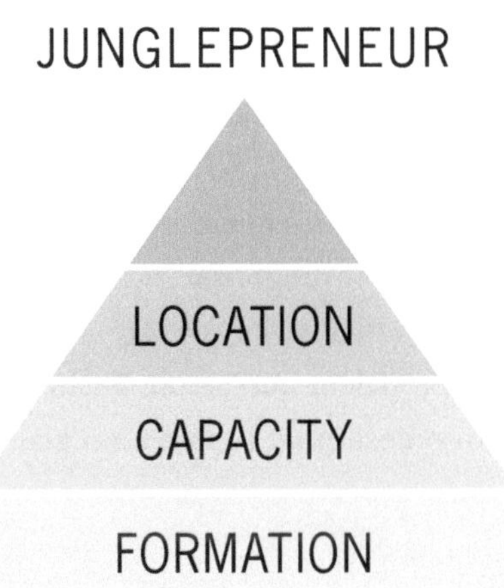

With the FOCAL Point framework, first the formation process of the Junglepreneur occurs in a unique way, similar to how precious stones are made. Rubies, amethysts, emeralds, sapphires, and diamonds are all very valuable in their own right, but their formation processes differ based on where in the earth's crust the formation took place and on the temperature and pressure they were exposed to during formation. These differences determine the type of precious stone formed and its value. Most precious stones of high value are formed in the earth's top crust at a depth of about 20 meters. However, the diamond, which is one of the hardest precious stones, is formed in the earth's mantle, which is much deeper and closer to the hot molten magma in the earth.[7]

Similar to the diamond's formation, the formation process of the Junglepreneur is extreme because tough business terrains can be likened to the deeper and hotter part of the earth's mantle. Since the businessperson in this terrain will be exposed to intense pressures and challenges in the course of developing the business, the journey of the Junglepreneur in these terrains will therefore build immense strength and resilience. Here is a case that underscores the importance of the formation process.

From Timber to Airlines: William Boeing founded the Boeing Airline Company in America in 1916.[8] William was previously involved in the timber business and also owned a shipyard. To succeed in timber he had to know which land was best for particular trees and then manufacture high-quality products from the timber. These all required a high attention to detail, efficiency, quality, and a certain level of perfectionism. So when William decided to get into the business of airplane manufacturing, these skills proved very useful. William had gone through the formation process in previous businesses and gained valuable knowledge and traits. He therefore emerged as a highly proficient and astute businessman who was able to pioneer Boeing into becoming the aviation giant of the future.

Boeing corporation has not only dominated the global airline industry but it has also become a key player in the defense and aerospace business sectors.[9] Boeing over the years has grown to become a multinational company of about 170,000 employees and with revenue of over $85 billion a year. The fact that Boeing is a corporate giant in the world today is a fitting tribute to the solid foundation laid by William Boeing. This also attests to the formation process he had to go through to become the person he had to be for the Boeing Airline Company. So the formation process is so vital, and the next case is also useful in explaining it because it is about one of the most successful female businesspersons in recent times.

Queen of Sales: Mary Kay started off by selling books door-to-door in the United States during the Second World War and then went on to work for various companies selling different consumer products. She went through the hard process of learning how to make the direct sale until she came to a point of excellence as a salesperson. In her previous places of work, she was passed over for promotions due to gender issues at that time, so she decided to start Mary Kay Cosmetics in 1963 with only $5,000 of seed money. By this time she understood the power of sales incentives and sharing success and had formed the resilience to see the company through the tough business of selling cosmetics directly to a large consumer market. When she died in 2001, her company had revenues of around $1.4 billion per year. Presently, Mary Kay Cosmetics has doubled that revenue and currently employs over 3 million sales consultants globally.[10]

The second distinction of the Junglepreneur is the survival capacity to excel in chaotic, unstable, undefined, or rapidly changing business environments. An environment with a high rate of change can be likened to a constantly moving goalpost in a soccer game. It will take a highly trained and skilled player to score into such a moving target. The story of the Toyota Motor Corporation and its founders is a case in point.

The Toyota Capacity: Kiichiro Toyoda had founded Toyota in 1937 based on the foundation of loom works started earlier by his father, Sakichi Toyoda. Eiji Toyoda, however, took over from his cousin and friend Kiichiro as president of Toyota in 1967. Before this time, a few years after the Second World War, Eiji as a senior executive had visited major American car manufacturers, and he noticed that the yearly production of Toyota was what some of the American competitors produced in a single day.[11] Furthermore, Toyota was operating in post-Second World War Japan, which was quite a tough terrain itself. It could have been easy for him and other senior executives of Toyota at that time to get discouraged with the rapidly changing car industry and chaotic postwar conditions. However, Eiji and others at Toyota progressively studied the weaknesses in the global car production systems for improvement opportunities and also focused on the advantages within their society, which included strong workplace philosophies. Over time they then developed the capacity to reduce waste, improve efficiency, and increase global production. They built Toyota to become a leading auto maker in the world.[12] If Toyota had not developed this survival capacity, it is unlikely that they would have achieved this level of success. Similarly, the Junglepreneur seeks to develop survival capacity and skills, which enables success in highly dynamic business environments.

The third key distinction is the location of the Junglepreneur in very tough business terrains. A useful analogy for this is to consider the plant world, where all plants belong to the same biological group. However, not all plants are of the same species. They differ based on their genetic composition, the habitat in which they are located, and the resources they have access to. Similarly, people who conduct business could all be grouped as businesspeople, but not all businesspeople are the same. Businesspeople also differ based on their genetic makeup, skills, available resources, and most especially the environment in which they have to operate. Specifically, the Junglepreneur is particularly adapted to operate in locations with harsh and unpredictable characteristics. This is just like a cactus has adapted to survive in the desert. Note that the cactus is a still member of the plant family, but it is very different from its temperate cousins, having evolved to survive moisture-deficient desert environments by extracting all the moisture from its own leaves and thereby turning them into thorns. Talking about plants, the case of the horticulturists offers an example of the impact of location on Junglepreneurship.

Blooms from the Horn of Africa: Ethiopia has had a history of difficult socio-political times and naturally is therefore a tough terrain to conduct business in. However, some horticulturists there led by Tsegaye Abebe, the then head of their national export group, defied the odds. They discovered that the Ethiopian terrain is very good for growing flowers, due to its high altitude and nutrient-abundant soil. So eventually overcoming the challenges in their tough terrain and maximizing the opportunities, they went on to develop a huge overseas market for their Ethiopian flowers. Now it is a $200 million-a-year business, employing over 55,000 people and also opening up direct air freight routes to major international airports.[13]

So these are the three unique distinctions of the Junglepreneur, as explained using Junglepreneur FOCAL Point. They can be influenced, developed, or formed from the outside in and from the inside out. The outside in are those influences such as resources, competition, market conditions, knowledge, and institutions that come from the tough environment and transform the Junglepreneur. The inside out are the internal traits that the Junglepreneur develops, like mindset, discipline, persistence, adaptability, and courage, which are used in the tough terrain. The Junglepreneur could acquire these internal traits from nature or from being particularly nurtured through personal-development activities, like participating in coaching courses. Either way these traits need to be purposefully identified, constantly perfected, and honed to very high levels in order to survive the tough business environment. The Junglepreneur cannot afford to operate such skills at average efficiency levels, as much greater levels of skill efficiency are required to succeed in tough business environments.

Diamonds

Above, we compared the Junglepreneur to a diamond, and talking about diamonds, the following story helps us to understand who the Junglepreneur is not. It will, however, try to set the stage for who the Junglepreneur should strive to be and also what the Junglepreneur needs to know.

There was once a certain businessman who lived in a large city and was doing quite well distributing consumer goods. Sometime later he became discontented and wanted to make more money, so he thought that diversifying his business would be appropriate. Then he heard about a new national business interest in precious stones and how people were making huge profits, particularly in the diamond trade. The businessman wanted a piece of it, and soon he heard about a major jewelry fair, which was going to take place in nearby city. Seeing this as a good starting-off point to break into the precious-stone business, he sold a warehouse full of goods and collected the cash for the purpose of trading precious stones. Before departing from his city, he asked around a bit about diamonds and was told that as long as he bought conflict-free diamonds, he would be fine. So he took his cash and left in search of opportunities in the jewelry trade.

The fair was full of glittering precious stones and various sellers in flashy suits and lovely dresses, and he asked around for which were the most valuable stones to trade. He was directed to the place where diamonds were being traded. There, a smooth and suave-looking seller began promoting his diamonds as "original flawless diamonds." The seller, who was quite savvy, soon caught the eye of the businessman, who thanked his good fortune for getting noticed so soon. The seller came over to him and handed him his business card, asking the businessman if he was ready to view the best-looking diamonds he had ever seen. The seller took him to a vast array of neatly arranged diamonds of all sizes. The businessman looked at them closely, and they sparkled like stars. He asked the seller his first question: "Are these diamonds conflict-free diamonds?"

"Sir, they were sourced from authentic sources, free from any conflict, and we have certificates to prove this," the seller replied.

The businessman looked at the seller and then asked his killer question: "Are they original diamonds?"

"Sir, they are original flawless diamonds and the best you've ever seen," said the seller.

So the businessman, feeling he had satisfied all due diligence procedures he knew for buying diamonds, immediately purchased all the flawless diamonds he could with his money. He got on the next plane and set off to another city he had heard was heavily trading diamonds so as to sell his flawless diamonds and make some very good profit. When he got there, he went to the leading jeweler and immediately announced he had original diamonds for sale. The wise, old jeweler with a full head of white hair was having his afternoon tea and gave the businessman a bored look. He slowly finished his tea and then asked to assess the diamonds. The businessman brought them out, held them up proudly to the light, and displayed them in all their glory. The jeweler put his eyepiece on and took his time to look closely at each diamond.

After a while the jeweler then set his eyepiece down, peered intently at the businessman, and announced to him that he had an offer. The businessman could not hide his excitement about the prospect of huge gains and asked what the offer was. The jeweler said, "I will offer you the cost of your airfare here for all your diamonds."

"What?!" said the shocked businessman. "My airfare is just a few hundred, while these flawless diamonds are worth millions."

The jeweler replied, "Well, you see, that is exactly the problem. Your diamonds are manufactured original flawless diamonds. However, what commands real value are natural diamonds, which often have a very small flaw or impurity in them, having evolved from a long natural process. It is the impurity that confirms if the diamond is real and of value, so these manufactured flawless diamonds you have are actually of very little value."

The businessman left in great anger and rushed back to seek the diamond seller and complain. He soon arrived back at the city and sought the diamond seller for explanations. The seller told him that he did mention to him that the diamonds were original flawless diamonds, and it was the businessman's choice to buy at those prices. He said the businessman should have asked for more explanations from him, carried out more diligent background work, or done a simple online search for information before buying. He said the businessman could even have consulted the jewel experts in the next row to get useful information about recognizing natural valuable diamonds, which always had flaws. The seller referred the businessman to the written conditions of sale and politely declined to refund the businessman any money, as he sold the flawless diamonds based on their actual state. There was little that the businessman could do, and his money was lost.

This true story depicts what can happen in the business jungle. It also raises questions that are relevant to many chapters in this book, as we will see later on. For instance, how could an experienced and relatively successful businessman make such a mistake and lose money? Could this mistake be because the businessman was overconfident, did not know the jewelry terrain well, and maybe even underestimated its toughness? Did the seller give false confidence or misrepresent the diamonds in an unethical manner? On the other hand, what happened to the businessman's vision and focus for his original businesses? Why did the businessman not conduct proper research or have a business plan before going into the diamond trade? It appears the businessman also got himself taken in by herd behavior, did not conduct proper risk management, could not handle manipulation, did not know the players, and had no team or network. These are some of the many issues that will be dealt with in this book.

Primarily, however, this story is again all about survival. The diamond seller and the businessman are both trying to survive and thrive in a game of wits, knowledge, skills, and tools. Finally, could it be that possessing or consciously deploying some of the traits of the Junglepreneur might have helped the businessman achieve a better outcome? This may be so, and issues similar to all these will be addressed in different sections of the book.

So in this first chapter, we have laid the foundation for Junglepreneurship, understanding who the Junglepreneur is and what makes the Junglepreneur distinct. In the next chapter we will look closely at the tough terrain that the Junglepreneur operates in. Even if you are new to harsh business terrains, distinguishing yourself by taking on board some of the concepts we've laid out in this chapter will make you the Junglepreneur.

Chapter One Takeaway: Junglepreneurs Required

- The Junglepreneur builds a business in any location and ensures its survival by staying creative, adaptable, persistent, aware, brave, linked, and energized—CAPABLE.
- The 2008 global financial crisis altered the business terrain, which will now be tougher, with new rules and players.
- The massive shift in global business will require Junglepreneurship as a survival-driven process to maximize all opportunities and overcome business challenges.
- Junglepreneur FOCAL Point is distinctiveness through formation, capacity, and location.
- The most capable beings will thrive and survive economically under the new law of survival.
- The Junglepreneur sees opportunities in challenges and prosperity in adversity.

Two
The Business Jungle

It goes without saying that when survival is threatened, struggles erupt between peoples.
—Hideki Tojo, Former Japanese Prime Minister

Don't wait around for things to happen to you by chance. Rather, engage your environment without fear, and dominate it to make good things happen every day.
—Samson O. Fasanya, Successful African Businessman

Both the jungle and tough business terrains are fascinating areas, as they have a life of their own and are also governed by rules required for surviving or thriving. The jungle is a paradox: full of dangers, yet at the same time full of huge rewards, opportunities, and resources. The jungle has plenty of prey and also loads of predators. The jungle can be noisy yet quiet, very beautiful and yet ugly. It can be very rewarding yet very frustrating, and it can be quite exacting and yet very fulfilling. All is not often as it appears to be in the jungle, and a nice, innocent-looking spot could have hidden within it very real and present danger. On the other hand, a tough business terrain is also a paradox. It consists of people, institutions, organizations, products, services, governments, currency, information, and resources. A tough business terrain can also be exacting and at the same time rewarding, frustrating at times and then exhilarating. It can be crushingly ruthless and yet also merciful.

In considering the jungle on one hand and the tough business terrain on the other, the overlap between the two can be termed the junglelike business terrain. Analogically speaking, within this central overlap of the junglelike business terrain is the essence of the Junglepreneurship concept. I have called this essence the Junglepreneurship CORE, comprised of Challenges, Opportunities, Resources, and Energy. This Junglepreneurship CORE is the foundation for the definition of Junglepreneurship itself, which I gave in the Introduction. I defined it as the survival-driven process of creatively maximizing all opportunities to resourcefully commence a business endeavor, overcome challenges, and thrive by using all legal means necessary. The Junglepreneurship CORE is depicted in the diagram below:

Junglepreneurship CORE

Looking closer into the Junglepreneurship CORE, we see its four components are a synthesis of the major areas that the Junglepreneur will need to tackle. First, the junglelike business terrain by its nature will present many challenges. These can be in the form of severe socio-economic inadequacies, extreme competition, funding shortages, deep market inefficiencies, over-regulation, and knowledge gaps, among others. In this terrain there are no alternatives but to overcome the challenges, and this is where the Junglepreneur can maximize the opportunities, resources, and energy present in that terrain. Every terrain, no matter how tough, will have opportunity gaps present, and these are discovered by the Junglepreneur through instinct, which we will discuss in more detail later in the book. Furthermore, irrespective of its toughness, the junglelike business terrain still contains a huge amount of resources, but in tough terrains the challenges often appear so daunting that the resources are sometimes either overlooked or missed altogether. This is where the mindset of the Junglepreneur plays a very important role. It helps to maintain the perspective required to tackle the challenges without discounting the opportunities and resources. In this regard, the personal traits developed by the Junglepreneur, knowledge of the terrain, and the networks available are also crucial sub-components. Finally, the energy in the Junglepreneurship CORE refers to the energy of the live species in the terrain and more specifically the energy of the businessperson. The ability of the Junglepreneur to generate, preserve, and deploy personal energy will be important to how the previous three aspects of the Junglepreneurship CORE will work favorably. I will be looking closer into all these sub-components of Junglepreneurship CORE later in the book.

The ability to overcome challenges and maximize opportunities and resources with a great amount of personal energy is what makes a businessperson succeed in any tough terrain. People like Sam Walton of WalMart, Sir Richard Branson of Virgin Group, Steve Jobs of Apple, Sara Blakely of Spanx, and my personal favorite, the West African street trader of the go-slow supermarket, all exemplify these traits. From this amazing group we will consider two cases.

From $5000 to $1Billion: The story of Sara Blakely's rise to success is quite inspiring. She had a seed fund of only $5,000 from her savings to invest in her business, and she used it to start a company which made unique female undergarments.[1] She overcame many challenges, including lack of interest by major hosiery manufacturers, until she found one who would make her exceptional products. Sara maximized all opportunities open to her and also invested a great deal of her personal energy, which she used to drive all aspects of the business herself, especially marketing. Started from her tiny flat, her company, Spanx, has gone on to become very successful, and Sara recently became the youngest female billionaire in the world.

From selling fax machines door-to-door to founding Spanx, the success story of Sara is quite inspirational and an example of what can be achieved with sheer determination. Her story is made even more unique because of her innate ability to somehow overcome challenges in a tough business environment and to keep going against all odds. This really is the essence of the Junglepreneurship CORE—the ability to survive and thrive when faced with huge obstacles or even when you do not seem to have a chance at succeeding. This next case is in a different context to Spanx but is nonetheless fascinating because on its own scale it is about doing what is required to overcome the odds.

The Go-Slow Traffic Survivor: The story of the West African street trader is intriguing. The street trader wakes up every day in daunting personal circumstances to face the business of the day. With little or no social welfare safety net in place by governing institutions to buffer against destitution, the street trader must brave the challenges from the barrage of natural elements like the sun and rain to maximize the immediate opportunities for making a living. In the eyes of the street trader, these opportunities lie in the slow-moving traffic on the highway and the potential buyers in the cars. Based on a beckoning signal from a potential buyer, the street trader with a burst of natural energy and high sprint speed—enough to rival world-champion sprinters—will chase down the car just to close that deal and survive for that single day. The street trader does this from sunup to sundown every day just to earn a few dollars. For the street trader, this is purely about survival; there is no other choice except being reduced to living on the rubbish dump. As much as any other, the street trader has earned a place of recognition.[2]

Junglelike Business Terrain

In many ways, tough business terrains can be likened to the state of the jungle, and in these scenarios, chaos and calm can almost reign side by side. In the jungle, the most unwholesome-looking plant or animal may actually be just what is required for survival or to take you to the next level. On the other hand, good-looking flora or fauna could turn out to be predatory or even poisonous. For instance in the sub-tropical or desert terrains, you can find fresh shrubs with fresh flowers, like the beautiful oleander plant (*Nerium oleander*), which only stays close to the few fresh water sources. The oleander flowers give off lovely colors in white, pink, violet, and red, and the sheer beauty of the flowers alone gives the impression that the water near it must be good or wholesome. However, the leaves, flowers, and bark of the beautiful oleander plant all contain cardiac glycosides, which are very poisonous to humans and animals. The glycosides in oleander are also water-soluble, which makes any water body close to the oleander plant bitter, undrinkable, and potentially fatal.

So in applying this analogy to the business jungle, sometimes all may not be as it seems. In business, an unlikely transaction or scenario could be the tipping point toward success, while a seemingly harmless proposition could become problematic. Often all that glitters is not gold. This reference to gold reminds me of some issues that Anglo-Gold Ashanti, the South African-owned gold-mining giant, has in some terrains. On the surface the company is in the enviable position of being an extractor of this highly sought-after metal. 'However, the company's past chairman, Tito Mboweni, spoke at the January 2014 economic forum at Davos about the challenges they faced from some locations outside of South Africa. He said that some of the locations were tough ecosystems that proved to be unnecessarily suspicious of their operations and lacked adequate infrastructure and supportive labor laws. In essence what they are facing is a tough, junglelike business terrain.[3]

Now let us consider further what we are likely to find in the jungle and in a challenging business environment. In the jungle you have all kinds of species and situations that exist there and play a vital role. These include herbivores, carnivores, flowers, fruits, birds, insects, rivers, trees, rain, drought, etc. It is very similar in the tough business terrains, which also have all types of players and scenarios: customers, competitors, regulators, honest people, unscrupulous people, business professionals, profitable situations, loss-making situations, etc. If you will look closely enough and discern based on your particular terrain, you may find actors, resources, players, and situations in the business world that occupy the very same roles as those in the jungle. However, the similarities you will find in this exercise may differ from that of another person, since individual terrains will differ. However, the Junglepreneur will still need to know how to handle the players and situations. In one way or another, your terrain will help to teach bittersweet lessons that will be vital to your future success.

Tough Places, Tough Times, Tough People

The business jungle that the Junglepreneur operates in does not have any particular geographic location. Tough business terrains are fluid and dynamic, and they can appear gradually or suddenly. They exhibit different characteristics, which can manifest in any location and sometimes with little or no prior indication. The table on the following page captures some of the characteristics of tough terrains and classifies them into categories. Please note that I have only given examples in this table as some pointers for identifying tough terrains, so the list of categories and characteristics is not exhaustive. You may yet find some aspects of your territory that I have not listed but you consider to be relevant to classifying your business terrain as a tough one.

JUNGLEPRENEUR'S CLASSIFICATION OF TOUGH BUSINESS TERRAINS[4]

CATEGORY	INHERENT CHARACTERISTICS
Economic	Regulatory problems, economic difficulties, sovereign debt default, recession, strikes.
Governance	Corruption, policy instability, ineffective government, repressiveness, lack of security.
Nature	Drought, typhoons, epidemic, famine, floods, earthquakes, other natural disasters.
Crises/ Catastrophe	Balkanisation, anarchy, terrorism, coups, violence, war, refugee crises, revolution.
Education	High illiteracy, dearth of information, inadequate research, poor funding, low skill levels.
Cultural	Age or gender discrimination, religious or ethnic discrimination, ideological imposition.
Socio-Political	Crime, poverty, societal depression, civil disobedience, disunity, nepotism, hegemonies.
Business Environment	Little support, low demand, high competition, oversophistication, scarce capital, skepticism.
General	Energy shocks, currency issues, food problems, failing infrastructure, weak legal system.

Now since I have been referring to tough business terrains all along, it is important at this point to differentiate between a tough business terrain and a normal business terrain. In this regard, a normal business terrain is one in which there are very few if any of the listed characteristics present in the territory. Even in cases where they exist, they are in mild forms, have a very short time span, or have very little or no adverse effect on the successful conduct of business. On the other hand, a tough business terrain is one in which any of these characteristics is fully present, has a long time span, and has a major adverse effect on the terrain. This then makes it challenging to conduct business and difficult to get successful results.

Some tough business terrains may exhibit a number of characteristics in only one category, while other terrains will have multiple characteristics in multiple categories. In such situations it will be a wonder that any business could exist at all. However, a business can thrive well even in very tough terrains.

Taming the Terrain: This is what African businessman Claude Ibalanky did in the Democratic Republic of Congo (DRC) between 2007 and 2012. The DRC has experienced a lot of turmoil in its recent past due to internal armed conflicts over power and natural resources, which have resulted in large humanitarian crises. Furthermore, in the World Bank Global Index for ease of doing business, the DRC ranks at the bottom of the table.[5] It was in the midst of all this that Ibalanky saw business opportunities. He established thriving businesses in DRC for the Bantu Investment Group, which he managed. The Bantu Group, a large business cooperative organization owned by thousands of South African labor union members, successfully established fast-food chains in Kinshasa, the capital of DRC, and achieved twice its estimated returns on investment.[6] While there, Ibalanky also helped the Group to establish plans to build massive electric plants and various manufacturing industries in the same terrain. He attributed his success in Congo to understanding the market, innovation, and adapting to the terrain.

However, it is important to note that tough terrains are not the exclusive preserve of countries where there is civil unrest. Tough business terrains exist everywhere, and even territories which appear to have relative stability also contend with a different set of issues. For instance, developed territories that rank highly on World Bank Global Index for ease of doing business have to contend with serious issues relating to growth. What could make these terrains become tough for firms and businesspeople is the extra effort required to achieve growth, extensive regulations, and shrinking profit margins due to sophisticated competition, high pace of business, and saturated or jaded markets. These circumstances create tough terrains even in sophisticated business environments.

In the e-commerce venture I co-founded in the UK, initially it was very difficult getting any retailer to sign on, and there were loads of rejections to deal with. This was probably because the pace of the market was so fast and no one seemed to have enough time. Our strategy was to persevere and continue to make contacts until someone listened. Eventually one or two retailers signed on. Then over time we had a portfolio of over 400 retailers to choose from, and the venture went on to do thousands of retail transactions. So tough terrains cannot be generalized or zoned, as every terrain has its own unique set of challenges that have to be overcome.

Stoic philosopher and Roman emperor Marcus Aurelius offers this piece of advice in his book, *Meditations*, saying: "If you are distressed by anything external, the pain is not due to the thing itself, but to your estimate of it; and this you have the power to revoke at any moment."[7] It does appear that some businesspeople have found this power to succeed in fluid, tough terrains through adaptability and perseverance. With this empowerment they have revoked the unfavorable estimate of their external business environment to survive and even thrive, despite the challenging circumstances in these terrains.

Nevertheless, the global environment of today does appear to have many of these circumstances existing throughout the world, creating difficult times for business. The present-day businessperson has few options when faced with tough terrains. While high-level educational training or business theories have their place, the businessperson may find that there is little preparation on the practicalities of handling some particularly challenging areas. I have argued that what is required are new ways of thinking, such as the concept of Junglepreneurship and its associated perspectives, one of which we will now consider.

Without the Box

In some places, the conventional business laws may seem to have been defied or somehow just do not apply. How to maneuver and tackle the various issues and challenges these tough business terrains will present may sometimes leave you in a dilemma as to what to do. Will your dreams vanish, or will aspirations be resigned to the belief that the present-day business world is just too tough and too volatile? To all these, it is the application of the new law of survival that will prepare you for the bumpy road ahead. Henry Ford once said, "When everything seems to be going against you, remember that the airplane takes off against the wind, not with it." So it will also require the Junglepreneur to reach deep within and without to find unusual qualities, tools, tactics, and techniques such as courage, vision, self-control, focus, and strategy to cope in tough terrains and take off against the wind.

This often requires a new way of thinking. *Thinking outside the box* is a popular catchphrase for management, used to typify thinking without limitations. However, for the Junglepreneur this may not be enough, as the box still exists, and its presence will be distracting. The Junglepreneur will need to discount the presence of the box by *thinking without the box* because accommodating for the existence of the box itself could still be a limitation due to its presence.

Production without Power: A soap manufacturer with a unique product that had been gaining popularity in the market found his business operating in a tough business terrain. There was a crisis in the national electricity supply system, and the infrastructure was severely stretched. Electricity was limited, erratic, and sometimes almost non-existent even to industrial areas. For days on end, there would be no public electricity, and in the rare cases when the electricity came on, it was supplied to industrial areas—against all rational logic—only at 5 PM, after most of the working day was spent. In such a bizarre, unexplainable situation, the manufacturer had to come up with a practical solution to save his fledgling business, since at the time he could not afford to buy private backup generators. So he reformulated the soap and redesigned his production equipment to come up with a simple system employing pulleys and gears, which allowed workers to use easy manual effort to get the production machines working. Effectively, the manufacturer no longer needed to rely on the public electricity supply at all. They successfully operated this way for many years until the business grew strong enough to afford backup generators, which were now only required to power their greatly increased production capacity.[8]

If this manufacturer had been thinking outside the box, he may have only considered his options from the onset as being limited to getting backup generators by all means or modifying the workplace schedule. However, because he was thinking without the box, he found a way to eliminate the need for electrical power altogether.

Terrain Unfamiliarity

It is important to also consider that tough business terrains inherently possess some form of unfamiliarity, which presents further problems to the Junglepreneur. Managing risk only adds to the pressures of the tough terrain. Often, the options are simply to quit or not to quit. This is a personal decision every businessperson must make, but in most cases the Junglepreneur will choose to continue the business venture in a practical manner and with the application of the survival philosophy.

Let us consider another story to give an analogy about an unfamiliar terrain. It was Christmastime, and the little three-year-old boy noticed that Mommy had been busy with that big green tree for a while. She had told him it was a Christmas tree, and she had covered it in sparkling lights, shiny tinsel, and a very large red-and-white stocking, which she said Santa had filled with goodies. Mommy soon departed after finishing the tree decorations, and the boy was left in this wondrous but unfamiliar world of flashing lights, brilliant colors, and enticing-looking materials. The boy decided to make some sense out of this unfamiliar scene. He was attracted by the large, lovely, red-and-white stocking, which seemed to be filled to the top. He dipped his hand into the stocking and discovered it was full of fantastic-looking shiny wrappers with something possibly edible in them. He unwrapped one of the pieces. It smelled lovely, so he put the brown thing it contained into his mouth. Yes, he was right; it turned out to be the most delicious thing he had ever tasted. So he took a few more and went back again a few hours later to have more still of what he would later know to be chocolates.

Some days passed, and soon it was Christmas Eve. The little boy went again to fish out another wrapper of chocolate, just as he had been doing for the last four days. He noticed this time that the stocking was not as full as it had been. Still, he would go for another one anyway. Just then his mommy walked in and was shocked to find him eating chocolates all by himself. So she checked the stocking and discovered to her great alarm that her son had just about finished the tub of small chocolates she had emptied into the stocking. A few hours later, the boy broke out in a rash all over his body and had to be treated for an allergy triggered by eating too many nuts from too much chocolate.

The boy in the story happens to be my own son, and thankfully his younger sister was too young then to follow him in this adventure. Though this story is about my little boy and chocolates, the main concept is analogous to finding oneself in unfamiliar terrain. He found himself in what would look to a child as a safe space, filled with innocent and sweet-tasting chocolates. However, he did not know that, despite the sweet taste and smell of chocolates, they should only be eaten in reasonable quantities. Unfamiliar terrains bear risk which is better managed based on information and experience. The Junglepreneur should not underestimate the business jungle but should approach it knowing that innocent but costly mistakes are possible if the necessary experience and knowledge is lacking.

As daunting as the terrain may seem, the Junglepreneur must know that business and financial success is also achievable in unstructured or unfamiliar environments. In unfamiliar terrain a Junglepreneur will take calculated risks to succeed, with a carefully planned, risk-mitigating, business execution and exit strategy. This is because great riches are often found in circumstances of unfamiliarity or uncertainty for those who have the heart to bear the pressure. It does take a person who has developed tenacity through training to go into a business jungle and succeed. Tough situations can bring out the best in you, however, and you can find hidden strength you never knew existed.

However, those who will survive and thrive in the business jungle will be those who are willing to come out of their comfort zone. These are Junglepreneurs, willing to use the necessary tools to do what it takes to survive and make it to success. With the right tools, the Junglepreneur can make reason out of unreasonable situations, make sense out of chaos, and create patterns out of seeming nonsense. Now stay with me because we are really about to get into what to do to become a Junglepreneur or how to become a better one, if you consider yourself to be one already. As the foundations for the concept of the Junglepreneur and Junglepreneurship CORE have been laid in these first two chapters, we will start considering from the next chapter some tools that I have developed. These tools will help you to map out how to overcome challenges, maximize opportunities and resources, and use personal energy to survive and thrive in any business terrain.

Chapter Two Takeaway: Junglepreneurship Essence

- The Junglepreneurship CORE is about overcoming challenges, maximizing opportunities, deploying resources, and using personal energy effectively.
- Tough business climates can occur in any geographic location and with short notice.
- Compared to a normal terrain, a tough business terrain has challenging circumstances present for a long time span and with major adverse effects.
- Challenging circumstances such as recessions, ineffective governance, or failing infrastructure can be found in the economic, governing, and socio-political aspects of a tough terrain.
- Instead of thinking outside the box, rather discount the presence of business limitations by *thinking without the box*.
- Tough business terrains inherently possess high levels of unfamiliarity that cannot be underestimated.
- Business and financial success is still possible in unfamiliar or chaotic business environments.
- Conquering tough business terrains requires deploying Junglepreneurship skills, knowledge, and tools.

Three
The Junglepreneur MINEKIT

Accept yourself, your strengths, your weaknesses, your truths, and know what tools you have to fulfill your purpose.
—Steve Maraboli, author of *Unapologetically You*

Abraham Maslow, a noted psychologist, once said that when a man has only a hammer as a tool, everything he encounters looks like a nail.[1] This comment aptly describes the challenges of not having the right range of tools or knowledge when faced with business challenges, and this is where we begin to go into the specifics of how to become a Junglepreneur. Knowing how to become a Junglepreneur or be a better one is really critical to your success in any location because taming challenging business terrains requires specific knowledge and skills. In this regard the tough terrain of the business world is like a gold or a copper mine, which could be located in the jungle. Such mines will throw up many impediments before you can successfully conquer them to get out the rich resources. Meanwhile, remember that earlier we defined the Junglepreneur as a person who can build a business in any location and ensure that it survives and thrives by all legal means, through staying creative, adaptable, persistent, aware, brave, linked, and energetic—or being Jungle CAPABLE. As mentioned earlier being Jungle CAPABLE means the Junglepreneur has the ability to actually tame any tough business jungle and to survive and thrive in it. However, to tame this type of terrain and live up to this description, the Junglepreneur will need to be properly kitted with the right variety of specialized tools.

Junglepreneur MINEKIT

Therefore, a unique set of tools has been precisely developed as a special terrain-taming toolbox I call the Junglepreneur MINEKIT. I specifically developed the Junglepreneur MINEKIT for navigating and taming business terrains, so that with it you are able to conquer such terrain in any location. The kit itself contains specific knowledge tools that address different key areas in strategy, management, and innovation that are especially required for your success.[2] The Junglepreneur MINEKIT has seven key components that are necessary for succeeding in any business terrain:

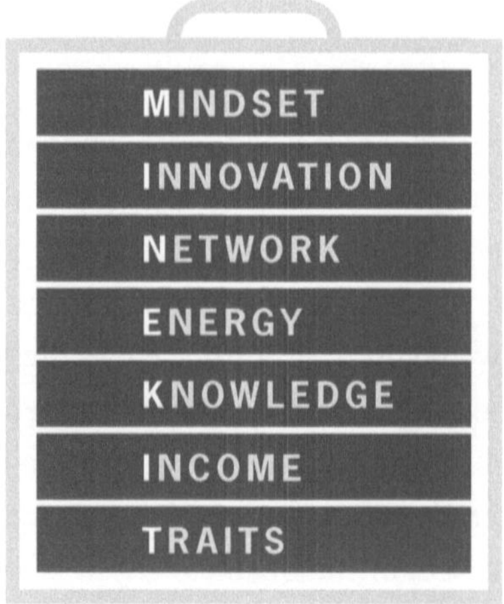

The *M*, which is for *mindset*, is critical to surviving in a tough business terrain because everything else is based on how you see your territory and the state of your mind. Despite the challenges that may exist in your terrain, if you can get your mindset honed and aligned in such a way that you see yourself eventually succeeding in that terrain, then you certainly will. So the mindset you have, the quality of your thoughts, and the way you perceive the territory will go a long way in determining how successful you will be. The next component, *I*, stands for *innovation* and complements having the right mindset. With innovation you can use what is available in that terrain to get what you want. The ability to innovate will be a determining factor for success in the present turbulent business terrains. *N* refers to your *network* in a business jungle and how you can leverage this for success. With *E* for *energy*, you are able to harness your strengths and maximize your personal potential to succeed in that environment. In any tough terrain, you need to have a certain amount of *knowledge* to successfully manage it, and this is the *K*. With this knowledge you can go into any business terrain and have a minimum level of understanding about what will be required to tame it. The second *I* is for the *income* that you need to earn as a measure of your success and for the continued sustenance of yourself and your business. Finally, your developed *traits* are the *T*, which is what sets you apart from your competition and also sets you up for success.

This is the composition of the Junglepreneur MINEKIT, and with it you can fulfill the new law of survival, which as you may remember, says that the most capable beings will thrive and survive economically and otherwise. However, to use the Junglepreneur MINEKIT for maximum efficiency, the Junglepreneur will first need to know how to use each tool. I liken this to a general training that a miner receives before engaging with mining tools and the mine itself. In the context of this book, things like direction, vision, focus, goal-setting, excellence, brain function and double-checking help make the task of using the Junglepreneur MINEKIT more efficient, faster, and smoother. So before delving into the details of the components of the Junglepreneur MINEKIT, let us first put everything in context. Then later on we will unpack the components of Junglepreneur MINEKIT and go into more details about them.

Direction and Compass

The worst thing that can happen in the jungle is not to know which direction to go. You will soon get lost no matter what you do. However, knowing how to use a compass and understanding the movements of the elements, like the Sun and the Moon, can help to map out where you are and find the right way forward. It is very similar in the business jungle. An analogy to describe lack of direction is, for instance, to have set up a ladder to climb a very high wall, only to reach the top of the long ladder and then realize you have been climbing up the wrong wall.

So choosing the right direction relates to deciding on your particular area of business interest. The compass is akin to the tool used in choosing or managing that business area. Likewise, the elements are reference guides against which you set milestones or goals. Choosing the right area of business will require you to identify work tools, personal skills, and abilities and tailor them to give you the best potential to succeed. The tools employed will be eventually determined by the area of business you choose.

Vision

Vision can have many definitions, but consider this business case, which best describes vision as it relates to the Junglepreneur.

From Short-Haul Passenger to Airline Owner: The son of a shipping tycoon had been involved in the family business with his father and older brother for a while and was doing well. They controlled a reasonable chunk of the global shipping market, but the younger son had a long-term vision to build a large business for himself. He wanted to be involved in an area of business where his family had no previous reputation—to make his own name outside of his father's shadow—but he kept this vision close to his heart. One day while he was on a flight, he considered the high airfare and wondered why he had to pay so much for a short-haul flight from London to a nearby European city. He felt he was being overcharged by the airline and then thought that if he felt this way, there must be many others who also felt the same way. So, since he already had a vision to be in business for himself, he decided then and there that his business direction was to start a budget airline, which would be affordable to all. He was inspired by the low-cost philosophy of WalMart stores and of Southwest Airlines in America, and he shaped the plan for his airline around this.[3] Soon after, this younger son, Stelios Haji-Ioannou, fulfilled his vision and launched EasyJet Airlines in 1995. EasyJet started with just two aircraft and commenced business as a low-cost airline, which made its margins by removing middlemen. It also worked hard at reducing other operating costs related to airline meals, staff uniforms, and other airline extras. EasyJet was thus able to provide a no-frills but safe and reliable airline service that the average person could afford. It all started from that simple but focused vision of owning a large business.

In addition to very hard work (Stelios Haji-Ioannou is reputed to work up to 16 hours per day), this vision empowered Stelios to build a very successful company. As of 2012, EasyJet employed over 8,000 people, had carried 58 million passengers to date, and was arguably the largest low-cost airline operating from Britain. EasyJet had 190 planes, 87 percent passenger load factor, revenue of £3.8 billion, over 600 flight routes, and 23 European operating bases. Stelios, as he is popularly called by investors and employees, had the overall personal vision to run his own business, and while pursuing this, he built an airline with a corporate vision to make "air travel as cheap as the cost of a pair of jeans." He says further in his own words, "It is not rocket science: EasyJet flies the same expensive tubes of metal as its competitors but manages to do it more cheaply, luring passengers away from the established airlines and making travel affordable for everyone, even those who had never flown before." Stelios's vision has redefined the airline and tourism industry in Europe for a long time to come.

So vision is seeing the desired end target of all that you want to do concerning your business. The Junglepreneur should clearly identify what is the corporate vision for the business or project and what is to be achieved from overcoming all the obstacles. Your vision must be a sharp, clear, detailed picture held in the mind with constant focus. Just like the vision Stelios had, your vision must be constant and must drive all actions and goals, no matter the present challenges or issues vying for attention.

Goals and Junglepreneur Task Tunnel

Goals and milestones periodically show you how far you have come in achieving the vision for your chosen business area. Goal-setting is difficult and comes with an inherent tendency for one to avoid it, ignore it, or procrastinate in doing it. However, for the Junglepreneur it must become an essential and regular activity.

The Junglepreneur simply has to learn to master the process of setting and achieving goals, as there is no way around it if you are to ensure lasting success. Goal-setting has many popular formulas, but the Junglepreneur needs one specifically developed to be very practical and easily applicable. So in developing this, an important micro-component of goals are smaller, more manageable tasks. The Junglepreneur philosophy holds that if the tasks can be successfully tackled consistently, then it is very likely that the larger goals will also be achieved. So in this regard, the Junglepreneur Task Tunnel has been created as a seven-step goal-achievement process developed with the focus on tasks as the route to accomplishing goals. It has been simplified here thus:

- IDENTIFY: Start with identifying all the known tasks necessary to accomplish the overall goals and vision, and then write them down in a format or location you can easily access.
- QUANTIFY: These tasks are the activities relating to your goals, so quantify the tasks in terms of the resources that will be required. The quantification should be in a form you can relate.
- COST: Next consider the physical effort and financial cost of carrying out the tasks to see if it is within reason. If not then you may want to reconsider the tasks.
- RANK: Next rank all the tasks in order of importance and prepare your Junglepreneur Task Tunnel. Your Task Tunnel is your action or to-do pipeline for passing a certain number of your tasks through and getting them completed.

- CHOOSE: Choose five or six of the most important tasks, have a simple plan to do them, and put them into the starting point of your Task Tunnel.
- DO: Take the first step exactly where you are, start doing your first set of five tasks, and get them moving along nicely.
- NEXT: Once the first set of five tasks are underway, choose the next set of five tasks. Start doing them alongside the first five, but spread all the work over a reasonable period of time.

At any time you should have about eight to ten tasks going in your Task Tunnel, but you will realize some of the first set of tasks are soon to be completed. Once your first set of tasks has been completed and the second is well underway, start a third set of tasks at the beginning of your Task Tunnel. At any point, you may decide to reduce the total number of tasks in your pipeline to a number you can manage. The principle is to simply have a continuous process of tasks being put through your Task Tunnel until you have completed all the tasks necessary to achieve the goals and thereby achieve the vision. These tasks are important to your goals, so go over them daily for evaluation and also to report and document challenges or progress.

Regarding goal-setting and achievement, it is instructive to consider two championship rowers from New Zealand, Hamish Bond and Eric Murray, who have dominated men's rowing since 2009.[4] The two made history in 2014 with the longest winning streak in men's international rowing events. They achieved this by winning 16 straight major titles in a row, including 10 world cups, five world championships, and an Olympic gold. The winning streak of the pair could be attributed to their goals regimen. The pair are known to first set out their benchmark goal for the year. Then based on this, they map out their monthly goals and filter these down to their daily goals. They keep their daily goals in focus, take each day as it comes, and do all they can to achieve their goals for the day every single day. No doubt it works for them, as they have their winning streak to prove it, and they say they are never tired of winning.

Focus

The business jungle can be a noisy place, with many things competing for immediate attention. It is a place with many actors all making a show of their prowess and abilities. Thus, it is very easy to lose sight of goals and be mesmerized or even overwhelmed by the successes and seemingly infinite abilities of others. It is also possible to be intimidated by the sheer size of the goal or obstacles that are meant to be conquered.

The business jungle requires a calm and focused approach. You must make time for quietly reflecting on the situations and options you face. This process strengthens the ability to focus intently on an issue, goal, or challenge until it is solved. Think of focus as a laser with many rays of light, harmless on their own, but which combine into one single powerful beam that can pierce through many substances. The same principle of focus applies to us when we congregate all our human abilities and resources into one place and direction for achieving a goal. It results in great power and momentum, a powerful force which will penetrate through any obstacle.

I have seen some African market traders who have honed the fascinating ability to be completely focused when counting cash, so much so that even if you are engaging them in a conversation, they will not respond to you in words. Rather they will use the next number sequence of the cash being counted to respond to you, while nodding their heads at the same time. This way they do not lose focus by missing out a single number in the sequence.[5]

It is important not to lose focus. All champions are human, and even the greatest of them trembles with trepidation when first faced with the obstacles to overcome to succeed. What makes them different is how they achieve focus. They block out all present distractions, channel all their energies in one direction, and take the action necessary at that point in time. They then ensure that they back up their focused action with belief that they are good enough to achieve victory. In most cases if the actions are taken regularly enough with great focus, they result in success, and the world applauds these athletes. The Junglepreneur is no different and can achieve immense success by learning to block out the distractions and focus on what needs to be done to succeed.

The Focused Flying Fish: Michael Phelps, the 27-year-old swimming phenomenon from the United States, is often seen coming out to the pool with a pair of large earphones covering his ears. He is said to use this not for just listening to motivational sounds but mainly to block out the noise from the audience so he can concentrate on the race ahead. Phelps, also known as the Flying Fish, was noted by his coach to be extremely focused, and through this he has achieved phenomenal feats in sports. At the 2012 London Olympics, he became the greatest Olympian of all time, with a cumulative 22 Olympic medals, out of which 18 are gold and all of which were won during the last three Olympics. In addition, Phelps has set 39 world records, was named World Swimmer of the Year seven times, and presently holds the record for the youngest swimmer to set a world record—set when he was just fifteen years and nine months old.[6]

Excellence

Excellence means ensuring one puts all one's personal ability, skills, talents, and intellect into every task that is required in the pursuit of the vision. Excellence results from putting all of one's heart, mind, and soul into every act, no matter how inconsequential the act may seem. Doing this will result not just in excellence but also in a kind of Midas touch, which enables one to succeed at almost everything. Excellence is a both a decision and an ability honed over time, and the Junglepreneur must cultivate this practice. The Junglepreneur must decide to adopt a spirit of excellence in everything, and by constantly carrying this out, the ability is further developed and sharpened until it becomes second nature.

Excellence may also be described as determining to do work only of the very highest quality. Aiming for this level of excellence may come at a cost, as quality and high standards have a price. Therefore, the costs of achieving excellence have to be weighed against the benefits. In the marketplace, for instance, the level of excellence being aimed at may also depend on the business strategy. If the business in question has a low-cost strategy, or the market competes mainly on price, then the strategic decision must be taken on how much the business will spend to achieve excellence. All the same, even a business that has a low-cost strategy will still need to have a minimum level of excellence displayed in its business. If not, it may not sustain customer loyalty. For instance, Ryan Air is a large, Irish low-cost airline operating in Europe and well known for its very austere approach to cost. Ryan Air, though one of the largest operators in the region, with revenue of over four billion euros, offers its airline services with no frills. However, at some point this may have begun to affect the quality of its customer service, as Ryan Air announced a profit decline of 29% in the first quarter of its 2013 financial year.[7] The company soon after announced that it was working on ways to improve its customer experience. So really there is a minimum level of excellence that your customers will expect.

On a personal level, excellence can be ingrained as a habit and developed in times of leisure. The Junglepreneur should seize every opportunity to practice excellence in all things and at all times. This is so that when the opportunity comes along that requires excellence, it will be displayed naturally when it counts the most. Pat Riley, the successful American basketball coach and executive, described excellence as what results from the gradual but regular attempt to get better.[8] So the habits and tasks that we engage with on a daily basis have a great role to play in achieving excellence. Therefore, how to achieve excellence involves the implementation of quality and high standards in our tasks and habits. Colin Powell, the former Chairman of the Joint Chiefs for the US Military and also former Secretary of State under George W. Bush, said, "If you are going to achieve excellence in big things, you develop the habit in little matters. Excellence is not an exception; it is a prevailing attitude."

The Brain

Neil Gaiman, bestselling fantasy author of *The Sandman* series and *American Gods*, once said, "All we have to believe with is our senses, the tools we use to perceive the world: our sight, our touch, our memory. If they lie to us, then nothing can be trusted."[9] The brain is that organ of the body trusted and responsible for mental capacity, cognitive function, concentration, memory, and aptitude. Since the brain is so important to the Junglepreneur, we will try to discover a bit more about one of the greatest parts of the human anatomy, whose immense capabilities are still being unraveled by man. The human brain weighs about 1.25kg (2.75 pounds) on average and contains up to 120 billion brain cells called neurons. Neurons are all interconnected to each other and also to other parts of the body. The brain uses these neurons to send out coded message signals all over the body in the form of small pulses, moving at an average speed of about 90 meters per second, using a mixture of electrical and chemical signals.

These chemical signals are what decide the actions of millions of nerves, muscle fibers, fluids, and vessels, which operate the human body. The chemical signals are released in the areas around the brain's neurons, called synapses. Each neuron in the brain has about a thousand synapses. So in essence, since the brain has about 120 billion neurons and each neuron has a thousand synapses, the computing power of the human brain is in the hundreds of trillions. The brain gives us memory recall, capacity, and ability, and it is where we react to all internal and external situations. So for the Junglepreneur operating in rapidly changing environments, the brain needs to be working at maximum capacity so as to ensure survival and success.

To carry out this massive computing-power function, the brain requires a lot of energy. The brain alone actually consumes about 18 to 22 percent of the total energy requirements of the entire body. This energy to be used by the brain is obtained from the foods and fluids that are consumed by each person. So it goes without saying that the quality of the functioning of the brain and its decisions depends a great deal on the quality of your diet. Just as important, the connections between the neurons are also strengthened for better decision making through increased use or mental exercises. Richard Bandler, a neuro-linguistic programming (NLP) proponent and author of the book *Get the Life You Want*, once said, "We need to learn to treat our own brain better—understanding how it works will help us do that."[10] Exercising the full functions of the brain should be a continuous activity of the Junglepreneur, including the constant development of mental capacity. Guides on developing the mental capacity can be found in the chapter on mindset in this book.

Double-Checking Your Double-Check

Amazing acceleration and deceleration tests were carried out in the USA during the 1940s. Since such tests could result in death, it was important then as now that every step of the complex experiments were checked and cross-checked various times. From his experience with the tests and the sometimes glaring errors discovered from pre-test cross-checking, Col. Stapp of the US Air Force coined the term *Stapp's Paradox.*[11] The paradox says that "the universal aptitude for ineptitude makes any human accomplishment an incredible miracle." Even though this description may be over-the-top, it does show that humans have the ability to make very serious errors. Humans are the most advanced and efficient creatures, but we also have an unbelievable capacity for mistakes that may prove costly. This is why the Junglepreneur must make sure to double-check everything and then repeat the exercise by double-checking again, or preferably getting someone else with a fresh pair of eyes to check what you have double-checked. In this process, it may be useful to always have an extensive list of the things to check for and then tick them off one after another as they are actualized. The list could even have its own built-in step-by-step process for discovering particular errors, but even that needs to be constantly double-checked to ensure nothing vital has been omitted.

The G-Man: Colonel John Stapp of the US Air Force was known as the fastest man on earth in the 1940s for his work on the effects of acceleration and deceleration (*g*-force of gravity) on the human body. By submitting himself directly for the tests using rocket-powered sleds, Stapp broke the known barrier of 18*g* (18 times the force of gravity), then known as the fatality limit for humans. He set a new record of 46*g* and helped to lay the foundation for a significant number of the flight and safety policies still being used by fighter-jet pilots to date. Furthermore, the test deployments pioneered by Stapp are still used today, and an unmanned sled achieved an unbelievable land speed of over 10,000kph (over 6,200 mph) in 2003—still arguably the world record for any land vehicle.

The double-checking your double-check process may be costly in terms of time and resources, but the benefits of preventing disaster may often outweigh the initial costs involved. The process is not a guarantee for removing all errors, but at least you will have significantly reduced the chance of serious mistakes occurring.

In this chapter we have focused on a range of intellectual tools. In conquering tough terrains, these intellectual tools should be used to prepare the Junglepreneur in using the tools around him. So in concluding this chapter on tools, let us consider what Winston Churchill, one of Britain's greatest prime ministers, was quoted as saying during the Second World War: "We shall neither fail nor falter; we shall not weaken or tire ... give us the tools, and we will finish the job." Having been empowered with intellectual tools, we will consider in the next chapter how the Junglepreneur can use them to succeed in the business jungle.

Chapter Three Takeaway: Components of Junglepreneur MINEKIT

- Become a Junglepreneur with a Junglepreneur MINEKIT, which is for navigating and taming business terrains in any location.
- The Junglepreneur MINEKIT contains specific knowledge tools and is comprised of Mindset, Innovation, Network, Energy, Knowledge, Income, and Traits.
- Have direction and choose a specific business area to ensure your business ladder is not up the wrong wall.
- Concentrate on your corporate vision for the business or project by constantly having a sharp, clear, detailed picture for what you want to achieve eventually.
- Use the Junglepreneur Task Tunnel to focus on your tasks as the route to accomplishing your set goals.
- Have a focused approach to the business jungle by congregating all your human abilities and resources into one place and direction to intently create a powerful force for achieving your goals.
- Put all your personal ability, skills, talents, and intellect into doing every task to the highest quality to achieve excellence. Engrain excellence through habit in times of leisure.
- Ensure your brain constantly works at maximum capacity by giving it enough energy from the right foods and adequate rest so it functions well to help you make the right decisions for survival and success.
- Reduce costly mistakes by double-checking everything for errors or omissions. Then repeat the exercise by double-checking again or getting someone else to double-check for you.

Four
Mindset and Innovation

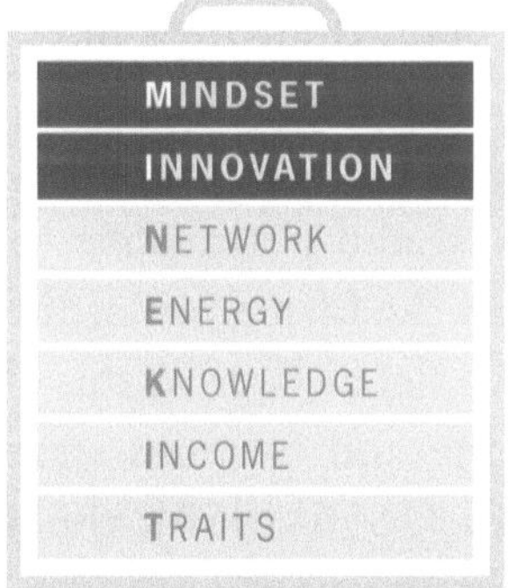

The energy of the mind is the essence of life.
—Aristotle

Mind is the Master power that molds and makes.
—James Allen, author of *As a Man Thinketh*

The first two critical components of the Junglepreneur MINEKIT are mindset and innovation, both of which will be considered here. Mindset operates in the realm of the human brain, which is one of the most complex human organs we have. Carl Sagan (1934–1996) was an author, a world-acclaimed cosmologist, a professor of astrophysics, and also the award-winning presenter of the popular television series about outer space, *Cosmos*. Sagan likened our brain to a muscle that we feel good about when it is in use.[1] The brain is also like a computer that runs software of various kinds. Our mindset, then, is the software running in the brain. The mindset is also the way the mind has been trained, wired, and programmed to act and react to different stimuli and situations. The mindset of the Junglepreneur is one of the most critical requirements to have success in any endeavor. It is vital that the mind runs the right software and operates the brain in the most efficient way. As author Daniel Amen says, "Your brain is the organ of your personality, character, and intelligence and is heavily involved in making you who you are … Your brain is involved in everything you do. Your brain controls everything you do, feel, and think. When you look in the mirror, you can thank your brain for what you see… Remember that your brain is involved in everything you do… every decision you make."[2]

Quality of thought, mental resilience, awareness, emotional intelligence, narratives, and perspective (or how one sees things) are all so important to the formation of the right mindset and will be considered in more detail later in this chapter. They determine the way we handle life and business issues required for success. George Bernard Shaw (1856–1950), the notable playwright, was also known for being the co-founder of the London School of Economics and the first man to win both an Oscar and a Nobel Prize in Literature.[3] He is quoted as saying, "One man that has a mind and knows it can always beat ten men who haven't and don't." So since the right mindset is what sets apart the very successful from the average person, it is then very critical that the Junglepreneur continually works to master this area. We will now consider some of the things that are required to develop an effective Junglepreneur mindset.

Hone Mental Abilities

The great physicist Albert Einstein said, "Intellectual growth should commence at birth and cease only at death." Intellectual growth and mental strength can be deliberately developed. Just like weight training builds and tones physical muscles, so can the Junglepreneur do mental exercises to strengthen the neurons and cells in the brain. The Junglepreneur must make efforts to develop the capacity of the mind to its greatest strength and potential. A well-developed mental capacity helps the Junglepreneur to think faster, deeper, and more effectively. This ability will serve the Junglepreneur well in the tough business jungle, where you need to be sharp and think on your feet. The Junglepreneur should make the decision to use part of his or her free time to develop the mental capacity and thinking process, as this is an ongoing exercise even for geniuses.

As generally known, the thinking process involves the reorganization of external stimuli, information, and ideas through reflection and mental effort to get meaning or understanding. However, people have different personal beliefs and underlying assumptions, which influence this process. Therefore each person will have different thoughts as their end result of this thinking process. The thoughts are the final messages that the mind plays to itself, so to get high-quality thoughts, the thinking process, including your underlying beliefs and assumptions, must be focused and pure. You cannot rise above your own thoughts, so therefore the Junglepreneur's goal must be to think in such a way as to achieve a level of high-quality, positive thoughts. Thinking about the future can bring great benefits; Bill Clinton, the hugely popular former US president who is known to always be forward-thinking, counsels us to "always think about tomorrow." He even included this in his campaign theme song.[4]

Stretch Thinking Capacity

To build mental strength and thinking capacity, the brain and mind need to be stretched and developed. There are various ways to develop mental capacity. Here are a few:

- Read high-quality educative books and magazines or watch educational documentaries.
- Play chess, scrabble, or cluedo, the detective game.
- Brainstorm on current business or social issues and engage in intellectual debates.
- Solve quizzes, crosswords, picture or logic puzzles, or Sudoku.
- Mind map by identifying linked patterns from your written thoughts on an idea.
- Do brainteasers like solving mathematics or deduction problems.
- Attend educational courses, conferences, or seminars, or learn a new language.
- Meditate or carry out deep, reflective thinking.

To really challenge your brain, you must constantly give it access to lots of knowledge, information, and puzzles. This can be achieved by doing a great many of the mental exercises just mentioned and more. The Junglepreneur should make constant commitments toward learning and—like Brian Tracy, the highly respected author, also said—"be a lifelong student. The more you learn, the more you earn, and the more self-confidence you will have."

Understand Thought Power

In developing the mind, the intricacies of the conscious and subconscious mind are phenomenal knowledge areas. The conscious mind handles a lot of thinking and processes the reality we are mostly aware of when we are up and about.

The subconscious mind, on the other hand, usually operates in the background but is active all the time, even when we are asleep. It is responsible for most of our creativity and deeply held beliefs. Now this field of human consciousness and thought as it relates to the brain is a highly debated field, and I have identified the two main streams.

The first is the more classical quantum theory of consciousness, which essentially argues that consciousness is the result of quantum gravity effects in microtubules, or the platforms for intercellular transport in the body cell structure. The second is the more recent but highly debated electromagnetic (EM) theory of consciousness (or the EM field theory), which argues that consciousness is an outcome that happens when the brain produces an electromagnetic field under certain criteria.

EM Fields: One of the main EM arguments in the very complex brain and consciousness field is by Johnjoe McFadden, a professor of molecular genetics in the UK. His argument is essentially that when a neuron fires an impulse in response to stimulus from another neuron, it will create a disturbance in the electromagnetic field, and so the EM field is a reflection of the information from the brain. This information from the neurons then coalesces to form what McFadden calls a "conscious electromagnetic information field," or a CEMI field, in the brain, of which what we know as consciousness is transmitted back to the neurons from the field itself. This consciousness, which represents the information in neurons, then communicates its situation externally in electromagnetic forms, which we know as thoughts. This theory further argues that the CEMI field explains how complex information couples with ideas to provide meaning, since the electromagnetic field is the unifying factor for all the information contained in billions of neurons.[5]

Other proponents of the EM theory like Susan Pockett, author of the book *The Nature of Consciousness*, go further to argue that the EM field is made up of a universal consciousness, which experiences stimuli and thoughts from all other conscious beings in the universe.[6]

If we believe the EM theory, then it appears that human consciousness and thoughts have even more power than we realize. The arguments of the EM theorists, however, have been criticized by proponents of the quantum theories of consciousness, who argue that there is no proof of the effect of EM fields on brain consciousness. Nevertheless, the fact remains that this field is very vast, and the realm of thought and consciousness is one of the last frontiers of knowledge, which is yet to be fully conquered by science. It is still developing, and the years to come will reveal more proven information about the power of human thoughts. For now, it probably is enough to know that human thoughts are extremely powerful and to keep learning about how to harness their enormous potential.

Develop Toughness

Toughness often starts from inside and originates from the spirit of a person before it manifests externally. Leading athletes and businessmen place a lot of emphasis on mental toughness and resilience as the key to winning. Bill Russell is a retired professional basketball player who played center for the Boston Celtics, leading them to eleven National Basketball Association (NBA) championships.[7] Russell also captained the US team to a gold-medal win during the 1956 Olympics and was named the NBA's Most Valuable Player (MVP) five times. Russell clearly knew the importance of mental toughness and once said, "Concentration and mental toughness are the margins of victory." Bill Russell was awarded the Presidential Medal of Freedom by President Barack Obama in 2011, and the NBA also recently renamed its NBA Finals MVP Award in Russell's honor.

We can compare mental toughness to being as hard as a rhinoceros or as tough as nails. A nail is one tough piece of iron, and it requires a lot of force to affect its natural state. The Junglepreneur needs to become as tough as nails by determining that it will take a lot for any situation to have the power to break your spirit. On the other hand, a rhinoceros is one tough animal and is known to be able to take any punishment nature can dish out. If you have been fortunate enough to get to see a rhino up close, you will notice that the rhino's skin is extremely thick, just like armor, and it takes a lot to pierce it through. The Junglepreneur needs to develop a thick skin too. Do not let anything or any situation get you down or take away your hope and enthusiasm. Even if something does get you down, ensure it is very temporary by pressing your internal reset button. Completely clear your mind of all negativity through heavy and sustained exposure to very positive stimuli.

Once you have done an internal reset, you can immediately bounce back with newfound positivity. If you are able to do this, after some time the subconscious mind takes this as your natural state of mind and will do all it can to ensure you achieve what you want. For instance, many well-known billionaires have faced bankruptcy, but some of them bounced back. For those who are still successful, they somehow found the rhino-like toughness inside or pressed their reset button and were able to come back stronger than ever. Alfred A. Montapert, philosopher and author of the acclaimed book *The Supreme Philosophy of Man: The Laws of Life*, cautioned, "Expect problems, and eat them for breakfast."[8] So make no mistake, the Junglepreneur will face tough times in the journey to success and will therefore need toughness and resilience to endure. How does the Junglepreneur prepare in advance for tough times that may come? This can be done by always having unshakeable hope for a greater future, belief in yourself, desire for success, and immense enthusiasm. All of these must envelop the Junglepreneur as a protective hardened skin, just like the rhinoceros, and as a steely interior, like the nail. If these attributes do not come to you naturally, then they can also be developed and groomed by undergoing coaching and training in the relevant areas.

Maximize Narratives

Narratives are simply stories we use to explain circumstances, join the dots, and give meaning to situations we encounter in life. Narratives are all around us, and they are very important to the formation of our mindset, as at any given time, someone somewhere is either telling or listening to a narrative. As Daniel J. Siegel, a clinical professor of psychiatry at the UCLA School of Medicine and Executive Director of the Mindsight Institute, wrote in his book *The Developing Mind*, "Our dreams and stories may contain implicit aspects of our lives even without our awareness.[9] In fact, storytelling may be a primary way in which we can linguistically communicate to others—as well as to ourselves—the sometimes hidden contents of our implicitly remembering minds. Stories make available perspectives on the emotional themes of our implicit memory that may otherwise be consciously unavailable to us."

In our everyday lives, we experience narratives being continually passed on to us as words, pictures, music, art, drama, video, dance, literary works, songs, and poems. We literarily live our lives based on narratives, and they shape how we view our experiences as we use them to investigate our past actions, analyze our present circumstances, and assess the future. Narratives can pass on both positive and negative messages in these various forms and through various media. Motivational narratives are the right kind of positive, encouraging, enhancing messages that you or others should feed your mind with. It is very important for the Junglepreneur to protect the mind from negative narratives at all times by assessing the quality and source of the narratives presently running in the mind.

Improve Awareness and Perspective

Have you ever driven down a road and been unable to recall doing so, or have you heard someone mention something to you just a moment ago and been unable to recall it? We sometimes live our lives on autopilot, especially when things are moving in a fast and frenetic pace, as would be the case in a tough business environment. This is precisely the time for the Junglepreneur to build a keen sense of self-awareness by paying more attention to what goes on around the immediate environment. The Junglepreneur must also be present in the mind by developing the ability to slow down and see things or hear things in the external world and perceive what the internal mind is trying to communicate. As Gordon Selfridge, founder of Selfridges, once said, "People will sit up and take notice of you if you will sit up and take notice of what makes them sit up and take notice."

Developing the skill of taking notice will enable the Junglepreneur to grasp important information that may have been missed and be consciously aware of everything being done or said. This process gives great recall and helps the Junglepreneur enjoy activities more. The Junglepreneur also become more adept at taking action and learns more about daily and business activities as a result of paying more attention.

This skill is what sets very successful athletes and sportspeople apart. Awareness enables them to see and hear what their competitors cannot perceive, and they tune in to their internal communication. These attributes can give them the vital edge to win. So the Junglepreneur must always be aware of what is going on in the external environment, where the operations of the business are conducted. The Junglepreneur cannot afford to go through life in a bubble, since bubbles at some point must burst.

A wild buffalo that stoops down to drink water from a river populated by crocodiles is always acutely aware of the immediate environment, simply because it is necessary for its own life preservation. The buffalo is always consciously watching the water and surrounding bushes to notice if a crocodile is trying to lunge out to grab it by the neck and drag it into the water for the crocodile's dinner. That is life in the jungle, and similar things do happen in business life too. Awareness is crucial.

The way in which we see the world forms part of our mindset. Our perspective is like a color-tinted window through which we see the world. People have different perspectives, and therefore the color-tints of our windows are often different. Therefore, we are likely to see the world differently based on individual perceptions of sights, sounds, experiences, and our own reasoning. Over time we all have formed different ways in which we view the world around us and all that is in it. They may have common themes, but each person's color-tinted view on life is individually different from another person's. Our life experiences are all uniquely different, and perspective is often formed right from our childhood experiences all the way to adulthood.

Understanding our perspectives and those of others is critical for the Junglepreneur to survive and thrive in the business jungle. It does go a long way in forging our mindset, and it is important to identify the window through which we view the world to see if it is the right or effective one. The good thing to remember is that perspectives can be changed if they are not suited to the environment, though it can be a difficult process. However, to achieve the right mindset, it is worth going through a perspective change if it is required.

Adopt a Helicopter View

Imagine being in a helicopter and observing all from above, giving you the ability to reframe what is seen. The helicopter viewpoint is the ability to change perspective or see situations from another perspective, which gives one the bigger picture from an elevated level. It means seeing everything from a higher vantage point that reveals all the minute details and components of the situation. This presents one with very many different visual angles and different images, which combine to give the whole scenario.

A helicopter viewpoint also involves the ability to reason from both abstract and real-life viewpoints and to ask the right questions in situations. This ability forms part of the mindset, and it gives one the power of objectivity. Objectivity comes by observing from a detached point of view, rather than seeing it from an involved perspective while embedded in the situation. The ability to switch to a helicopter viewpoint is a strategic ability and critical component of the Junglepreneur mindset. It is vital to success in any endeavor.

Achieve Panic Control

When an emergency happens and a rapidly agitated state of mind or panic sets in, a person may fail to act or to decide in the best, safest, and most reasonable manner required to handle the situation at hand.

The ability to control panic is a mindset quality that very successful people have learned, which enables them to think through very serious situations that would have been otherwise devastating. Though it is very difficult to achieve when faced with a situation, the Junglepreneur must never, ever panic, despite whatever pressure the situation brings.

It is said that a quiet mind is best for getting a proper perception of the outside environment. So in a panic situation, the Junglepreneur must be able to achieve a serene state of mind within an instant in order to think very clearly and very quickly for the best solution to the problem. The Junglepreneur must train to achieve this serene state of mind, which will not panic but will think clearly in a tight situation. Since panic is a killer, one of the ways to control it is by quickly calming your nerves through various techniques. One of the techniques used in achieving serenity is mind preparation during normal daily situations. In this case the Junglepreneur finds opportunity on a daily basis to constantly tell the mind never to panic, until the subconscious mind gets the message and will speedily calm the nerves in any situation. Another technique is the ability to carry out immediate controlled deep breathing or instant shock treatment administered through quick, sharp slaps on your wrist.[10] When a deer from the forest wanders onto a highway and is caught in the headlights of a vehicle quickly moving toward it, panic is what causes the freezing of its mind. Since its mind freezes in fear and confusion, the deer's muscles also freeze into inaction, and the deer is subsequently hit. You must learn to deal with panic and always keep your wits about you.

Manage Emotions

Emotions are formed in the mind and are influenced by the person's personality type, physical state of being, and experiences. Since emotions are mental feelings, they do form part of a person's mindset. However, emotions can also be spontaneous, overwhelming, and sometimes triggered by external stimuli. Due to the important contribution of emotions to one's mindset, the Junglepreneur will do well to learn to identify the exact set of emotions that are being experienced at every point in time. This is even more important in tough business terrains, where your emotions can be easily affected by the wildly ranging external stimuli.

Identifying emotions in yourself is one thing, but learning to manage those emotions properly to achieve the right mindset is quite another. Managing the emotions well comes through sustained practice of controlling our spontaneous reactions, which could result from our immediate feelings. This could involve exercises like deep breathing, pursing your lips for five seconds, forming mental images of the consequences of your actions, or counting to 10 before responding based on emotions. It requires discipline and consistency to do any of these exercises instead of spontaneously responding to situations, but getting it right will keep the Junglepreneur on an even keel most of the time.

Alongside managing his own emotions, it is vital that the Junglepreneur learns to identify and manage the emotions of other people. Other people are important to the achievements of the Junglepreneur, and their emotions or mindset will have an important role to play. The ability to succeed with managing personal emotions and those of others is now being recognized as a type of intelligence. It can be identified through what is now known as an emotional quotient, EQ, which, along with emotional intelligence itself, are now made popular by the work of Daniel Goleman.[11] Goleman himself is quoted as saying, "If your emotional abilities aren't in hand, if you don't have self-awareness, if you are not able to manage your distressing emotions, if you can't have empathy and have effective relationships, then no matter how smart you are, you are not going to get very far."

Aspire toward Innovation

Innovation is the first *I* in the Junglepreneur MINEKIT, and developing the capacity for creative innovation is vital to succeeding in the jungle. Aspiring toward innovation means doing something entirely new or reinventing an old product or service. It means thinking in a different way from everyone else and doing things in a unique way or with an unusual twist.

$3.2 Billion for Innovation: An instance of innovative thinking is the digital, intelligent, and Wi-Fi-enabled thermostat and smoke detector developed by NEST Labs. Tony Fadell, the co-founder and CEO of NEST Labs, once remarked that "frustration is a great source of innovation." Fadell actually attributed the development of these products to the frustration he experienced using the traditional form of thermostats and smoke detectors while building his new home. From a home garage he then formed NEST Labs in 2010 with his partner, Matt Rogers, to further develop such innovative products. Fadell is someone who would be familiar with how worthwhile creative innovation can be. He is one of the people who developed the iPod while at Apple, and during his career, he has helped to develop over 300 registered patents. Fadell's NEST Labs has grown monumentally since its founding; the company was sold to Google in early 2014 for $3.2 billion dollars in cash.[12] Google paid this princely sum because it intends to benefit from the innovation excellence at NEST. Not a bad outing so far for a company that started from the simple but innovative idea of reinventing a thermostat.

NEST Labs demonstrates the value of creative innovation, which is also the ability to see things from a different perspective, or from another plane, and to go beyond what is the bar or limit of productivity and excellence. Furthermore, creative innovation means redefining current realities in the light of what could be and harnessing or reorganizing resources to create immense value for the society. The fruits of creative innovation are all around us—the automobile, the personal computer, the iPhone, etc. These products of innovation have brought tremendous value to the quality of our lives, while in some cases also generating huge revenues for the innovators. Stimulating creative innovation can be achieved through practice and, among others, will involve the following steps or processes:

- Think differently by always challenging the norm through asking *Why* repeatedly. Question why things are the way they are continuously until you begin to come up with new ideas.
- Practice concurrent thinking in different time slots and from different perspectives. In doing this, consider things from the positive, negative, collaborative, or fresh perspectives.
- Concurrent thinking allows you to see things from a more holistic vantage point, and thereby it is possible to notice something new or unique.
- Identify barriers to new ways of doing things which have become embedded into thought and practice. Constantly think of how you can break through the barriers or redefine the rules.
- Practice tackling impossibilities in your thoughts. Think of a list of things that you or others might consider impossible, and then ask why and how these things are impossible.
- Imagine each impossibility vanishing and you realizing the best possible outcome. Then think of what it would take to make it happen. You may find they are not actually impossible after all.
- Seek new perspectives through other people, who will see things in a different way than you.
- Become objective by practicing suspending your judgment until you get to a stage in which you can freely imagine all options.
- Focus your attention continuously on new or fresh things until you can find out what makes them different. This helps you to hone your ability to spot innovations.

The Junglepreneur is a creative innovator by nature, but you must also seek to develop this ability to its maximum potential. Making money in any terrain requires tapping into the future to supply the present with genius. An example of this is the creation of an unusual pastry by Dominique Ansel, a pastry chef in New York City. A cross between a doughnut and a croissant, both of which have huge followership among pastry lovers already, the Cronut became an instant hit in America, with long queues of customers waiting every day for the limited number of this unique pastry produced by Ansel's shop each day.[13] Due to this demand, some savvy customers even created a black market for it; some have resold theirs for as much as $40 a piece. The advent of the Cronut is due to the power of creative innovation, and developing this ability will require stretching the mind beyond the normal realm of thinking.[14]

We have considered the Junglepreneur's mindset and innovation in this chapter, and we will proceed further with another component of the Junglepreneur MINEKIT in the next chapter.

Chapter Four Takeaway: Facets of Mindset and Innovation

- Achieve the right mindset by training your mind to react to different stimuli and situations in an effective manner.
- Develop your mindset through reflection and thinking positive, high-quality thoughts.
- Stretch your thinking capacity through brainstorming, puzzles, mind mapping, meditation, etc.
- Become tough, and develop a thick skin to challenges. Achieve this by maintaining your desire, enthusiasm, and hope in your greater future. Don't let anything or any situation keep you down.
- Protect your mind from negative narratives always and at all cost. So constantly ensure your mind is only running motivational narratives with the right kind of positive, encouraging, enhancing messages.
- Take notice and be constantly aware of what is going on in your environment, and ensure you see things with an effective perspective.
- Seek the ability to achieve detached objectivity so you can see other aspects of a situation. Do this by assuming you are in a helicopter, and imagine the viewpoints you can get on the situation from an elevated level.
- Avoid panic; manage your own emotions and those of others well.
- Aspire to creative innovation by doing something new or reinventing something old. Also redefine current realities in the light of what could be, and harness or reorganize resources to create value.

Five
Network in the Business Jungle

It is no use saying, "We are doing our best." You have got to succeed in doing what is necessary ... Success consists of going from failure to failure without loss of enthusiasm.
—Winston Churchill

Our greatest weakness lies in giving up. The most certain way to succeed is always to try just one more time.
—Thomas Edison

The *N* referred to in the Junglepreneur MINEKIT is the network of the interactions or linkages between you, other people, and the business terrain itself. This means managing yourself, understanding others, knowing the players in the terrain, discovering what makes the terrain tick, and then being able to negotiate your way through. You are the one to fit all the parts of the network together, so let's start with you and what you need to know and have. First, the personal attributes you require for succeeding in the business jungle include being smart, savvy, aware, and tactful. Secondly, every terrain has features that guide the level of power and influence that is brought to bear. So the Junglepreneur must be adept at building a power base by knowing what's going on, whom to talk to, and which groups to support. Thirdly, the Junglepreneur's access to resources, knowledge, expertise, or influence—alongside being trustworthy, reliable, and dependable—are all useful in the process of consolidating a network for succeeding. In consolidating this network, it is important to understand that success and failure are interlinked, as there is rarely one without the other. Since it is unlikely that some level of failure can be avoided, it is then important that we commence the full considerations on network with how to deal with failure. Moreover, since the fear of failure needs to be conquered to succeed in the business jungle, we will deal with this now before moving on to the subcomponents of the network required for success.

Conquer Failure First

To build your network, you will need to project a good level of enthusiasm and vibrancy. This will be difficult if the feeling of failure continually crops up and becomes an overriding focus due to ongoing or past challenges. This could constitute a stumbling block toward building and consolidating a good network and business in your terrain, so it is necessary to look closely at this subject.

> The author Laurence Shames described success and failure as not really being opposites but more like companions, with success as the hero and failure as the sidekick.

Failure is real and can be very sensitive or traumatic, thus eliciting feelings such as shock, resentment, confusion, embarrassment, denial, and maybe even loss of confidence. Sometimes in trying to manage these raging feelings, one may try to find reasons to excuse the failure, explain it away, or even link it to something unrelated that gives some kind of meaning to the failure. However, though it may sometimes feel like a catastrophe, do not be afraid to fail; failure is part of the success process. Consider that you only need to succeed three out of five times to be successful and succeed four out of five to be outstanding. Embedded in these success scenarios are also one or two instances of failure. So failing really is part of the process of succeeding, and sometimes experiencing failure over and over again helps you to lose the fear of failure once and for all. However, in this process, it is also important to find out any underlying reasons behind failure so you can correct and eliminate these. This way you begin to reduce the cycle of failure till you eventually succeed.

The process can be lonely, as failure is said to be an orphan. That is, no one associates with supposed "failures"; they tend to be shunned or isolated. In reality, most successful people developed the personal capacity for excellence during their periods of quiet isolation. So if a person is isolated during a temporary period of failure, then it is a fantastic opportunity to build up personal capacity. If you complete the whole process and cycle out from failure into success, you build immense confidence. Should you face similar situations in the future, you can keep going, knowing that you will eventually succeed. Understand that in the pursuit of a goal nothing is totally lost when you fail. Each failure encountered is more valuable experience gained and simply another step on the ladder toward success. Sooner or later the missteps of failure will lead to success.

Failing builds immense resilience and tenacity and often results in a more rounded and experienced person. If or when you fail at a goal or task, it is very important that you never ever see yourself as a personal failure. This is very critical, as the minute you do so, a negative mindset comes in. Then the failure that should have been just another step to success becomes personal and permanent. From then on, it is game over. Learning from failure is the best way to maximize its benefit. When you fail, you have the opportunity to fine-tune everything required for excellence the next time around. For the Junglepreneur who learns to tame failure, success is inevitable. Just like General George S. Patton, the famous American WWII general, said, "I do not fear failure. I only fear the 'slowing up' of the engine inside of me, which is pounding, saying, 'Keep going. Someone must be on top. Why not you?'"[1]

Having considered the issue of failure, we will now look into some resources, activities, and abilities required to consolidate a network that will help you succeed in any environment.

Know the Players

Every terrain has a set of people who influence and determine what goes on there, whether one is aware of them or not. So the main process of building and consolidating your network starts with identifying these terrain players, what they do, how to reach out to them, and what you can mutually achieve together. The ultimate aim is to get these players to become part of your network. Your network also begins with the immediate and extended circle of people that you know directly. So who you know, how well you know them, and the positions of influence they hold are vital keys to your success. Therefore it cannot be overemphasized that the Junglepreneur has to build a robust network of people in all walks of life and in different spheres of influence. In building this network, there should not be any discrimination in whatever form; to succeed and survive, the Junglepreneur needs all kinds of people—from the security guard to the CEO.

Building your network also includes looking out for the different players in your terrain who have some forms of useful skills or know-how at various levels. You can measure the extent to which the players have these by considering the results they have achieved so far. Next find out a bit more about them by asking around. Know what really motivates them, and decide if their beliefs or values are in line with your own personal values. The next step is a symbiotic process of mutual benefit, and it starts with you deciding on the actual players with whom you have similar values. Then consider if they can really help you achieve your vision and what their motivations would be for doing so. To truly make it a symbiotic process, you should then consider the people whom you have just identified and get to know which of their goals you can help with.

The next step involves gaining access to these people by reaching out to them directly or, better still, going through someone whom they know and respect. Use the access wisely, and prepare in advance, as the first contact is usually the most important one necessary to establish a relationship. If a successful relationship is established, work on maintaining and nurturing it through regular communication and acts of genuine support and sacrifice.

> Pierre McGuire, a Canadian-born former ice hockey player and coach, made a comment which aptly describes this section, saying, "There are people who might complain about the so-called old boys network. My advice is to become part of the network. Volunteer to help; get involved. Hockey people tend to take care of hockey people."

The network you build and become part of will take care of you as you will of them. This is a natural social process that is sometimes neglected but really works.

Know the Score

Next in consolidating your network, it is important to know the score in your environment, what really matters or makes it tick. By this I mean that in every terrain there is a vision, major goal, overall agenda, or master game plan that has been put together and is known to the few players that control or influence that terrain. In some cases the game plan may not be easy to decipher or even directly related to your business or to you. However, you can be sure that it will certainly affect your way of life. Consider this simple story about a boy, his bike, and his aunt.

On a particular day, a teenage boy had ridden his bike well beyond his home neighborhood. As he turned around and pedaled frantically to get back home, he wondered to himself how he had managed to ride as far as the highway. *If my parents get to know, I'll be in big trouble*, he mused. Just six months ago, he had been given this brand-new, shiny, blue bicycle by his parents as his 13th birthday present. He was warned to limit the use of the bike to the small roads around their home, since the major highway adjoining the estate was deemed not safe for riding bikes. He had always kept to the rules, but today he had let his mind wander and had ridden too far. Just then a familiar voice called out his name, and he stopped riding to see who it was. He looked back, and to his horror, he saw his dreaded Aunt Alice just a few yards away, giving him a quizzical look.

Aunt Alice was notorious in the family for her mean-spiritedness. She beckoned for him to come close. She barraged him with questions about why he was riding by the highway and if his parents knew about it. The boy promised it would never happen again and pleaded with her not to tell his parents, as they would take away his prized bike. Aunt Alice gave him a long, nasty look and then promised not to tell his parents. When the boy got home, his cousin came to visit, and the boy told him what had happened. His cousin warned him not to expect much from Aunt Alice, as he had been caught up in unnecessary trouble with her many times in the past. Later that evening, Aunt Alice showed up at their house with a mischievous look, and true to type, she straightaway reported the boy to his parents. The boy explained to his parents what had happened and that Aunt Alice had already scolded him and even promised not to tell. His parents were furious with their son all the same, and the bike was seized for some weeks.

Very many years later, the boy, who had since grown into a man, asked his father about that particular incident. His father laughed and said, "Oh, your Aunt Alice had been trying to get on our good side because she had a business project she wanted us to fund. We decided not to fund it for the very reason that she still reported you, even after her promise. She couldn't be trusted, but you still had to be punished for breaking our rules."

Imagine that I had to lose my cherished bike because of my aunt's game plan. Yes, I am the boy in that story, and it was a shiny, blue

Raleigh Chopper bike, which to me then was equivalent to a sports car—so I was really upset. Of what significance could a boy and his bike possibly have to a project? However, that simply was the score: my Aunt Alice was using my bike incident to try to appear to my parents as if she cared so they would play along with her game plan for funding a business project. I have long since forgiven her anyway, and sometimes I still have a good laugh with my cousin about those troubled times with Aunt Alice. We also wonder what game she might be up to now.

Though it did not look like it at first, the unspoken game in this simple bike story was eventually revealed as a business project an aunt was trying to get funded. So it is the Junglepreneur's business to always know the score by being aware of the underlying reality that makes his or her environment tick, what the agenda is, how the game is played, what the tally is, and what the stakes are. Knowing the score is important so that the Junglepreneur's business is properly positioned for success—so long as the overall game plan remains legal and ethical.

Understand Personalities

In the previous sections, we have considered how you can build your network by conquering failure, knowing the terrain players, and knowing the score. However, people are a vital aspect of all these, as people are very important to success. So it will be very useful to understand the different personality types of the people around you and equally important to also know your own. The key thing is to understand people and their motivations, fears, aspirations, dreams, and expectations—what makes them tick. Having a good idea about personality types will empower the Junglepreneur to relate well with people, make the right judgment calls, and arrive at effective decisions regarding people.

Knowing yourself also through self-study of your own emotions, dominant thought patterns, moods, motivations, reasoning processes, and aspirations is a further key to success. The investment made in understanding personalities will really help you to understand yourself much better, particularly your own temperaments and why you behave in the ways you do. Now, human personality is complex since it relates to the mixture of human thoughts, acts, and emotions, which form a distinctive pattern of behavior for each person. It has been studied in many fields of knowledge, especially psychology, and thus there are many schools of thought regarding human behavior. Out of these there are those that can be considered as the grand old models. For instance, Sigmund Freud's psychoanalytical theory seeks to explain human personality as an interface of conflicting forces that operate in the various levels of human awareness.[2] Then there is the Raymond Cattell 16-Factor personality model, which argues about dual dimensions for each personality.[3] However, the Henry Murray theory of needs proposes that human personality is fashioned by different types of needs, such as the needs for power, financial gain, affection, or achievement.

On another hand, Erik Erickson's psychosocial stage personality theory considers the personality or ego identity as being formed based on the knowledge of self as experienced from social interactions.[4] Then regarding human development as it impacts personality, the socio-cultural theory by Lev Vygostsky believes that parents, careers, peers, and culture help to shape human behavior.[5] There are also recent arguments in the field of neuroscience that seek to debunk the left-brain and right-brain personality psychology school. For instance, some neuroscientific proponents argue that the parts of the brain are interlinked, while sympathizers of classical theories still continue to make their own arguments in an ongoing debate.

This wide range of theories, arguments, and models goes to show how complex the human personality really is. However, though there are so many theories and also new knowledge, some of the old models still provide a very good basic foundation for understanding this complex field. Here are a few to consider:

Friedman and Rosenman's Type A, Type B Theory: In 1959 two cardiologists, Friedman and Rosenman, found out that people with a particular type of personality, called Type A, had a higher risk of high blood pressure and heart disease than another type of personality, called Type B. Their theory describes left-brain-dominated, workaholic, high-strung, competitive, status-conscious people as the Type A personality types. The right-brain-dominated, steady-working, creative, relaxed, intuitive, reflective, moderate, and easygoing people are described as Type B personalities.[6]

Big Five Personality Framework (OCEAN): This theory was developed by researchers Costa and McCrae in 1992. This describes a personality trait and its behavioral pattern and then includes the exact opposite of it for comparison. OCEAN stands for Open, Conscientious, Extrovert, Agreeable, and Neurotic.[7] They are further described below:

- Open: Inventive and curious personality. On the flip side of an open personality is a closed personality, which will be consistent and cautious.
- Conscientious: A conscientious person is efficient and organized, while the opposite is a non-conscientious person, who may be just easygoing or even careless.
- Extrovert: An extroverted personality is outgoing and energetic, while the opposite is an introverted personality, which may be reserved and loves solitude.
- Agreeable: An agreeable person is compassionate and friendly, while a disagreeable person may be cold and unkind.
- Neurotic: A neurotic personality is likely to be nervous and sensitive, while a non-neurotic personality is confident and secure.

Hippocrates Personality Types: This initially consisted of four personality types as originally developed by Hippocrates (460–370 BC), but it was later refined into the five personality types by modern-day researchers.[8] They are now known as:

- Sanguine: These are outgoing, impulsive, friendly, and charming people. They often have short attention spans and can also be overly effusive. They may, however, be driven by a deep need for attention. They hurt easily and will not handle rejection well.
- Choleric: These are goal-oriented, strong, and capable leaders who get things done. They inspire confidence and respect in others, and their opinions are highly valued. They may also be overbearing and bossy and have a tendency to use people.
- Melancholic: These can be fearful, dull, and introverted people who are very happy with their own company. They may not be fun to be around but are often diligent. They love routine or repetitive tasks and are consistently dependable.
- Phlegmatic: This set of people may be seen as lacking drive, motivation, and ambition. They often may come across as also inactive and slacking. Fear of failure may often be the reason for this. However, on the other hand, they can be fiercely loyal, open, and easygoing.
- Supine: This group often has low self-esteem and is driven by a need to be liked by others. They may go out of their way to serve and do things for others. On the other hand, they can be tough if crossed and may be quite vindictive.

Whichever model is used from the three described, it should give a good basis for the Junglepreneur to start the never-ending but interesting process of trying to understand people better. These models are very useful in predicting human behavior to a great degree, which could be a tipping point during business meetings or crucial negotiations. This predictive ability also helps the Junglepreneur to become empathic by being able to see issues from another person's perspective, based on the understanding of their personality. Just as crucial, these models also help Junglepreneurs to better understand their own personality traits.

Negotiate Everything

With knowledge of human personalities, the Junglepreneur is better equipped for negotiating within the terrain network, where usually value is the commodity. Like time, money, resources, contacts, and skills, value is a created asset that can be exchanged for goods or services, and so it needs to be maximized. A wise Chinese proverb says that when you go to buy at the market, you do not first show your silver. So in consolidating your network, you must analyze and negotiate anything that requires parting with any form of value. Since you will be faced with many situations in your network in which value is at stake, you therefore need to be at the top of your game in this area. Note that when negotiating, one must not be intimidated by the other party but should continually haggle so as to get close enough to the other person's price limit. A saying goes that you are very near getting the best deal when you come close to being insulted. What happens often in give-and-take negotiations is that in reality both parties will usually be just slightly displeased about the outcome and often come away with a little bit less than they expected. Win–win is a popular desired outcome in negotiations, but in reality win–win situations are rare.

> In the jungle, for instance, can the predator lion and the zebra prey have a win–win situation? Imagine the lion negotiating with the zebra that it will only kill the zebra but not eat it. Or imagine the zebra negotiating with the lion that even though it escapes the lion, it will offer only its thigh as compensation.

In most deals or scenarios, especially in the business jungle, one party will always have the slight upper hand even if it is not very obvious. It is more a case of *you win some, you lose some*, and the goal of the Junglepreneur is to have more wins than losses through perseverance and hard work. However, the Junglepreneur who loses temporarily should not sulk but try again, while the Junglepreneur who wins regularly must be gracious about it yet never rest on his or her laurels.

Manage Yourself

Finally in building and consolidating the network, the emotions and experiences of the Junglepreneur will be at play and cannot to be ignored. How the Junglepreneur manages this aspect will be critical to successfully creating a network in the business jungle. Being a self-driven businessperson trying to start or grow a business network can really be a daunting task, and there will be a whole range of positive and negative experiences and emotions that one will pass through. From personal experience, there is the realization that the thoughts, heartaches, triumphs, aspirations, ideas, concerns, disappointments, achievements, trials, and vindications of the Junglepreneur may sometimes be difficult to articulate in words. Therefore, expressing them to some others and getting those people to understand where you are may be a challenge in itself and can make the journey a very lonely one. There will be times when the Junglepreneur will feel the weight of this pressure. But know that you are not entirely alone, even if it appears like you are. One of the things that can help during this time is to have access to someone very experienced in business or life in general. This person will allow you to talk freely about all that's on your mind or may just listen objectively and without any judgment. As you experience this rollercoaster of emotions, look around you closely. You may be able to find at least one or two people you can access who will be willing and able to listen to you or offer useful advice.[9] In addition to connecting with the right people, it is even more important at these times to connect with your higher belief for encouragement, wisdom, direction, and hope. These steps can make all the difference and will help the Junglepreneur to find stability during periods of turmoil or uncertainty.

Having considered strategies for building and consolidating your network, have no fear about your ability to succeed in any tough business terrain. If you work hard on implementing even just a few of the Junglepreneur MINEKIT concepts we have learned so far, you will succeed. However, there is yet more exciting stuff to learn in the following chapters, which will help you succeed even better.

Chapter Five Takeaway: Network Keys

- Your network is made up of linkages between you, other people, and the business terrain.
- Build your network by managing yourself, understanding others, knowing the players, knowing what matters, and being able to negotiate.
- Grow and influence your power base in the terrain by being savvy, aware, and tactful.
- Start building your network by first conquering failure through learning from your mistakes, never seeing yourself as a failure, and by understanding it is all part of the success process.
- Develop your network by knowing the key players in your terrain, values you have in common, and your mutual benefits to each other.
- Understand personalities so you can relate with people, know what makes them tick, and thereby make the right judgement calls.
- Maximize your network by negotiating anything that requires parting with any form of value, as it is always at stake in the network.
- Consolidate your network by successfully managing your emotions and experiences, which are also at stake in this process.

Six
Your Energy

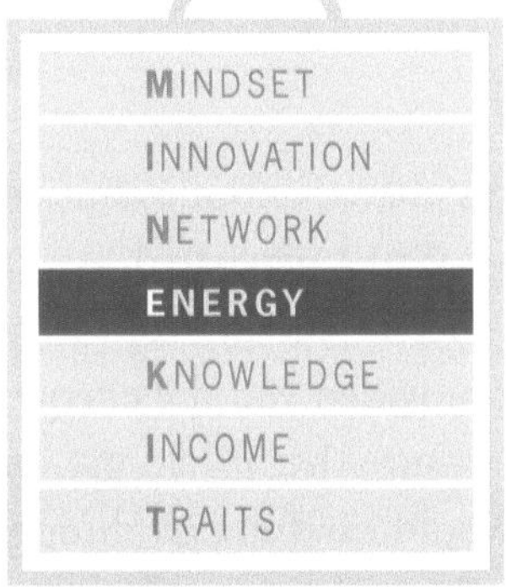

All our dreams come true if we have the courage to pursue them.
—Walt Disney

Obstacles don't have to stop you. If you run into a wall, don't turn around and give up. Figure out how to climb it, go through it, or work around it.
—Michael Jordan

E is all about your personal energy and how you are able to harness, preserve, and deploy it toward succeeding in your terrain. Your energy is central to all aspects of the Junglepreneur MINEKIT, to the Junglepreneurship CORE, and to being Jungle CAPABLE. It drives all three. With the right level of energy, you can take on the challenges in your terrain and maximize all the opportunities and resources. The new law of survival emphasizes that the most capable beings will thrive and survive. However, this law too relies on energy for it to be accomplished. Concerning survival, the famous movie producer Danny Boyle says, "That survival instinct, that will to live, that need to get back to life again, is more powerful than any consideration of taste, decency, politeness, manners, civility. Anything. It's such a powerful force."[1] Yes, survival is such a powerful force, but without energy it will be difficult to survive. So the Junglepreneur must always remember that, for as long as it is about survival, then it is also about energy and how to generate it, preserve it, and use it effectively. These three aspects will be the focus of my discussion.

Generating Energy

Without personal energy there is no movement and no progress, so it is important that energy is first generated. Assuming you had a power plant and wanted to generate energy from it, you would go through some steps to ensure it provided you the energy effectively and consistently. You would first ensure that it had gas, oil, and other necessary inputs, and then you would carefully go through the proper sequence for starting the power plant. If you used a wrong sequence, then it is likely the power plant would not start or it would malfunction later. Now your body is one of the most sophisticated energy-producing systems existing, so to similarly generate energy from your body, you are expected to do some basics like eating well, resting, taking plenty of fluids, and exercising regularly. However, there is one more important step for generating and maintaining your personal energy, and this is starting your body system in the right sequence.

Get out of Bed Free

This sequence for generating your personal energy starts when you get up in the morning. The sequence involves the Junglepreneur ensuring to start each new day on a positive and powerful note, as this is critical to building up energy right from the beginning of the day. Even if you don't feel like it, you must start the day with energizing positive thoughts or affirming statements first. You must get out of bed free from negativity, and this starts immediately when you open your eyes, or at that very first instant of consciousness when you wake up. The second you wake up, start to think only of positive things to be grateful about; the first is that you even woke up safe and sound that day. You could also immediately start to speak out affirming words, like telling yourself how blessed you are, what a wonderful day it is, how you can achieve anything, how the day is yours for the taking, and so forth. Note that when one wakes up in the morning, there is the tendency that the first thoughts that may flood to the brain are negative or discouraging thoughts. This could be a carryover from current circumstances. Even in this case, it is still critical that the Junglepreneur get out of bed on every new day immediately free of all negativity by making every effort to think positive thoughts and make motivating statements.

After getting your first thoughts and words right, the next thing to address early in the morning is your body metabolism. Knowing that metabolism is how your body breaks down nutrients to get energy and uses this energy to fuel the cells of your body to produce more energy, it is then important to address it first thing in the morning. You do this by giving your body metabolism a boost in the morning with some exercise, deep breathing, breakfast, and drinking fluids, which preferably should be water for your maximum hydration.[2] It is acknowledged that people do have different eating habits; however, unless you are abstaining from food and fluids for religious, health, or personal reasons, it is useful to eat some breakfast and drink water in the morning to enhance your energy level. I also mentioned the exercise and deep breathing because it helps to get more oxygen into your system, and this is a vital requirement for efficient metabolism.[3] You can carry out deep breathing by consciously noting the level of air you are taking in. If you feel it is shallow, then take in more air by filling your lungs and belly and releasing in a continuous cycle for a few minutes.

Even if all these steps are done in just small volumes, they help your body and mind to be free from lethargy and negativity and commence the process of generating energy for your body right from the morning. It is important to note that during the day, your energy levels will vary or may even dip due to the demands on your body based on the different physical and mental activities you do. Therefore you can maintain and replenish your energy throughout the day by constantly monitoring your thoughts, feeding, hydration, and breathing to ensure they are in line with the good standards you had set in the morning. Do all of these consistently from when you get out of bed in the morning till the day runs out, and you will be free to succeed in your terrain, as the difference in your energy level will be very clear in a matter of days.

Preserving Energy

Furthermore, since energy is also what gives the Junglepreneur strength to think, take action, be motivated, and succeed in the business jungle, it will be necessary to consider how to protect and preserve the energy you have diligently generated from the morning and maintained through the day.

Avoid E-Killers

The major step toward protecting your energy is to be aware of what I call *E-Killers*, or energy killers.

> An E-Killer is anything that drains your personal energy in a sudden or gradual manner. An E-Killer can be anything, anybody, or any circumstance that causes a regular negative effect in you. E-Killers are those things that constantly make you unduly feel one or a combination of the following: tired, discouraged, unproductive, lethargic, or anxious.

Without energy, business projects cannot be achieved and visions cannot be realized. An energy killer will drain your energy, so the Junglepreneur should avoid E-Killers like the plague. Sometimes it is people who unfortunately allow their weaknesses or challenges to make them act as E-Killers to the Junglepreneur either knowingly or unknowingly. If people who act in this capacity cannot be avoided, then interaction with them must be limited. Epictetus, a Greek sage and philosopher who lived between AD 55 and AD 135, is quoted as saying, "The key is to keep company only with people who uplift you, whose presence calls forth your best."[4]

How to avoid or manage E-Killers starts with being able to properly identify them, and a good way is for the Junglepreneur to carry out a personal energy level audit on a daily basis. You do an energy audit by simply checking if your personal energy and enthusiasm is above average, within average, or below average throughout the day, based on what you know about yourself. After the audit, if you notice a decline in your energy or productivity, then take particular note of the circumstances around you recently which may have caused the energy loss. This way you can begin to identify what the E-Killers are with respect to you. Alternatively, after carrying out your personal energy audit, you may have noted a surge in your energy or enthusiasm, and if you can identify the recent circumstances that caused this, you can replicate it when needed.

Handle Manipulation

In protecting or preserving your energy, it is necessary to address the subject of manipulation because, though it can be subtle, it also has the potential to use up a lot of your energy in trying to deal with the situation. Now manipulation for survival is not unusual, and it can be a natural instinct of all creatures. For instance, whales and dolphins manipulate circumstances in their favor when fishing for food. Whales will go after a large school composed of thousands of fish swimming very closely together in a synchronized manner. These schools of fish are known to usually move very swiftly in tight formation and multiple directions, which makes them difficult to catch. The whales' strategy is to give out a special long, high-pitched sound targeted at the school of fish, which is so tightly knit that it looks like a moving ball. This unusual sound confuses and disorients the ball-like school, and the whales use the sound to slow the fish down and change their direction. By this time the whales have the very slow-moving ball of fish exactly where they want them. The whales then slam the near-stationary school of fish with their massive tails, knocking unconscious a large number of the fish. Finally, the whales move in to pick off the fish individually.[5]

In the case of dolphins, many actually collaborate with humans to get what they want. At certain islands in the far eastern part of the world, dolphins are known to herd large schools of fish close to seashores where they know fishermen will be waiting with fishing nets. When the dolphins have herded the fish close to shore, they will show the fishermen where the large schools of fish are by slamming their tails in the exact spot where the fish are located. The fishermen then move in to throw their fishing nets in the water. Some fish are caught in the tight nets, but other fish escape and are now separated from the school. The isolated fish then try to escape on their own, and these are the ones the dolphins go for and catch easily for their meal. So, in essence, because the dolphins cannot hunt a large, close-knit school of fish, what they are doing is using the fishermen to help separate the fish they can catch.[6] Now if whales and dolphins can be intelligent enough to be so manipulative, you can then imagine the potential of humans to manipulate others.

In the business jungle, you will find that people try to influence others to do what they want for various reasons. Some of the reasons for influencing others could be for mutual benefit, while other reasons may not be entirely selfless. When people try to cause others to do their own bidding, irrespective of the actual desires or needs of the person being influenced, this is pure manipulation and could be a huge drain on the energy of the person being influenced. So in the business jungle, manipulation will be encountered in various forms, which could be direct, indirect, open, or subtle, and in yielding to manipulation, a lot of energy can be unnecessarily dissipated. So for survival and energy preservation's sake, the Junglepreneur needs to know how to deal with manipulation. The following process should help:

- Recognize: The first step is to be able to recognize manipulation, and the Junglepreneur can do this by closely analyzing the actions or inactions of others.
- Take Note: Always ask yourself again about the true motivations of others regarding their dealings with you, and note their behavioral patterns.
- Take Care: If you find the motivations of others to be absolutely selfish, vengeful, or negative in many ways, then take serious care.

- Think Long-Term: Consider the long-term nature and effects of the actions and inactions. Some forms of manipulation look innocent enough in the short-term but are actually long-term plans which will unfold later.
- Find the Network: Always trace the actual source of the actions or inactions of people secondary to you. A master manipulator may use your colleagues, family, and friends to try to manipulate you without their realizing they are being used.
- Backtrack: Note the real issues and backtrack to the source by probing with questions. Also carefully consider if the present communication pattern of a secondary person to you is consistent or if it is strange or unusual.
- Identify: If it is inconsistent, strange or out of pattern, then it may be influence of a third party coming through the secondary person close to you.
- React: In the end, decide how to react to manipulation. In some situations you may have to strategically decide to play along in your own best interest. At other times it may be best to nip the manipulation in the bud immediately.

The most important thing is that you must be aware of manipulation if it shows up and ensure you are the one with the power to decide how it will play out. It is important to also note that manipulation in the long run most often backfires and will also require a lot of energy to execute it, so the Junglepreneur should try to avoid doing it to others.

Seize the Morning, Seize the Day

Once you know how to protect your energy, it helps to know how to maximize all that preserved energy for greater productivity. There is an old adage that goes, "The morning is the day, and those that will see goodness must make the most of it." For the Junglepreneur the morning of a new day starts at midnight and not when one wakes up much later, since in reality each day does actually begin at 12 AM. All creatures on earth have 24 hours in a day to pursue their needs, and humans are no different. Humans, however, have the capacity and ability to best utilize the 24 hours of time that we are all given. There is a common business saying that "there just aren't enough hours in the day." However, on the contrary, those that go on to become very successful were not given more hours in the day but have simply mastered how to use time and energy more productively and see time in the right perspective.

One way to do this is to see each of those 24 hours as individual bars of gold that you are given each day as your starting working capital. The Junglepreneur must see each hour of the day as a separate valuable unit, a chunk of time that must be used wisely. Each hour of time is actually worth much more than the value of a gold bar if one knows how to utilize the time well. Out of the 24 gold bars of time we are given each and every day, the most valuable set is usually the first eight hours, between 12 AM and 8 AM. I do understand that you can be productive at any time of the day depending on your circumstances. Also it is known that different people experience peak productivity at different times of the day and, irrespective of your blocking time out in the first eight hours to work, you will still be expected to do productive work at some points during the rest of the day. However, those first eight hours are important for the following reasons:

- It is the time most people are asleep or just stirring for the day. The Junglepreneur can use this undistracted time to work on personal goals or targets.
- During this time your energy is not being dissipated through other activities or distractions, so you can thus deploy your full energy toward more productive tasks.
- There is less noise during this time, and it is a great period to carry out prayer, meditation, or spiritual exercises.
- At this time the Junglepreneur is free to think clearly without interruption or interference. Many great inventors, leaders, and thinkers have used this strategy successfully.

- There is less atmospheric pollution at this time of the day, so the air is fresher. At this time, the Junglepreneur can practice breathing deeply to feed the brain with high-quality oxygen required for optimum brain functionality.
- It is a very quiet time within the 24-hour period. Great inspirations and ideas for creativity often come during very quiet times.

I have indicated that the most productive time of the day is often the first eight hours, so it is suggested that the Junglepreneur must find the discipline to block some time from this slot to be awake and alert and to maximize the most from them. Depending on your individual natural body rhythm and sleep pattern, the time chosen in this slot need not be much, as even one hour will make a lot of difference to your productivity and results. Doing this will create unbelievable momentum for the achievement of goals, visions and dreams. This book itself is a testament to what can be accomplished in the first eight hours of each day, as I often blocked time out of this slot to find motivation to write or think through my ideas. It is very important also during these first few hours of the day to watch how the time is spent or what goes into them. What goes into this time often sets the tone for the rest of the day.

The Junglepreneur should avoid the temptation to spend this high-quality time on checking emails, worrying, social networking, spontaneous internet browsing, or casual entertainment. Most of these can wait for later in the day, as this high-value time should rather be spent on some of these: thinking, strategizing, working on your goals, writing, exercising, creative work, reading, or carrying out other important tasks required to set you apart for excellence. President Franklin D. Roosevelt's wife, Eleanor, the longest-serving American First Lady (1933 to 1945), was popularly known then as the First Lady of the World. She loved each new day and has been quoted as saying, "With the new day comes new strength and new thoughts."[7] So, like Eleanor, love and seize the day.

Manage Herd Behavior

In nature, animals of the same species often tend to bunch together into a massive herd, triggered by the actions of one another and able to decide to energetically move in one direction at the same time. Sometimes this is irrespective of whether it is the right direction or not. In the business jungle, herds can be described as groups of people making similar business decisions. Being part of a social or business herd, as the case may be, can be useful as part of the survival strategy of the Junglepreneur. Furthermore, there is group energy generated that can be useful in helping to push forward individual goals. However, a herd can also dissipate a lot of energy if not managed well, and so it is necessary to understand it. If well managed and understood, a social or business group can provide the Junglepreneur with common support, synergy, information, communications, protection, and joint goal achievement. It really can be beneficial to be in a herd if there is a common goal or when facing a mutual business predator, as numbers can overwhelm, making it difficult to single out anyone who stays within the herd. However, the key to the Junglepreneur being successful in a herd or group is to know the purpose for being there, keep a clear head, and keep one's eyes and ears open.

Apart from losing energy, it is important to also bear in mind here that there can be danger for the Junglepreneur in being part of a social or business herd that is out of control—this can lead to serious problems. Notable American economist and former Assistant Secretary of the Treasury Edgar R. Fiedler once said, "The herd instinct amongst forecasters makes sheep look like independent thinkers."[8] The reason for this type of comment by Fiedler is because uncontrolled business herd behavior has been known to causes many economic depressions, financial market meltdowns, and business losses like the recent one of 2008. This is simply because of the effect of group thinking, where the basic fundamentals of the decision being taken were either not cross-checked or were ignored. If the social or business herd is then seen to be blindly moving in the wrong direction toward a catastrophic cliff and potentially wasting energy, then it will be necessary for the Junglepreneur to first warn the herd and then leave the herd and go off separately for the sake of survival. The Junglepreneur can know when to break from the group by always checking the fundamentals of the underlying decisions. Rational reasoning is often the first casualty of herd behavior, so if the fundamentals don't support sound logic and rational reasoning, then you should think critically about whether to continue with the herd or not. Simply put, to save your energy, if the fundamentals don't check out, then you should check out of the herd.

Have Backup Plan Z

When things go wrong, a lot of energy is consumed trying to save the situation, so it is better to have an alternative plan or better still to prevent things going wrong in the first place.

> Murphy's Law says that "if anything can go wrong, it will." This maxim is credited to Major Edward Murphy, a US Air Force engineer working on the aerospace deceleration project in 1949. Murphy's Law was deemed to have been partly responsible for the success of the project, as it was their desire to prevent this law from occurring in their aerospace deceleration project.[9]

Often we try to ensure that we have a backup plan in case something we do not envisage happens, and having a backup Plan B has been the usual route. However, the popularity of having a Plan B is long over because it is no longer practical. This is because, due to the rate of turbulence in the business terrain at present, one or even two backup plans may not suffice, and you will lose energy trying to figure out another solution if your initial backup plan fails. So to preserve energy, the Junglepreneur, rhetorically speaking, should have a Plan B, Plan C, Plan D, Plan E, and even up to a Plan Z. The idea is to have as many backup plans as may be required to be prepared for most eventualities and save precious energy that would be lost if things went wrong. The Junglepreneur must always hope for the best but prepare for the worst of the worst. So ensure you have backup plans to the backup plans of your backup plans. Though this may be an expensive or costly option in terms of resources, the multi-layer level of preparation ensures the

Junglepreneur will at least find one way out if faced with a dire situation. Hopefully this should be enough for most eventualities, and if it is not, then at least you did try your very best to plan ahead.

Deploying Energy

I have been addressing ways to generate and preserve energy, but what do you then do with all the energy you have generated and preserved? You deploy this precious energy for progress toward accomplishing your goals by creating value, generating movement of your goods and services, securing your precious assets, networking, and spending time with loved ones for your personal fulfilment. Let us now consider these.

Create Value and Mobility

A very good use of your energy is to channel it into the creative process by harnessing all your full potentials, resources, and opportunities and transmuting them into value. The creative process is really very energy-consuming, and so it is a great way of utilizing your personal energy for always creating value in one form or another. Creating value could be by providing goods, services, inventions, or knowledge that will really enhance the lives of others and contribute to the general progress of society. After creating value, you then need mobility, which in this context refers to moving your goods and services from one location to another for the purpose of transacting business. Ensuring this occurs efficiently is a useful deployment of your energy. Aside from this initial definition, mobility for the Junglepreneur also means international access to all the major business countries in the world either through physical means or through communicative means. Ensuring your own efficient mobility is also a good use of your energy because moving around and communicating freely means the Junglepreneur can meet the people vital to success and make the most of business opportunities as they emerge.

In another sense, mobility also means that the Junglepreneur can energetically keep moving forward in the direction of goals and visions. In a real-life jungle, even if you are a veteran and know what you are doing, still you can never underestimate its dangers and opportunities, and so you have to keep moving. Likewise in tough terrains, irrespective of the experience level, the Junglepreneur needs to keep moving forward so as to stay ahead of challenges and to maximize opportunities. Energy enables you to do this.

Create Linkages and Achieve Your Goals

You should also use your energy for the vital networking process, which enables you to connect and keep in touch with all the people and institutions necessary for your success. The amount of energy required to do this cannot be underestimated, and so it is an important and effective use of energy. Next you need to spend some quality time with loved ones, which may involve different activities that will require your energy. If you are the very busy type, your loved ones will really cherish the time you spend with them and will want your full attention. Without good energy levels, it will be difficult to do this. Then of course you also need energy for yourself so you can do the activities that give personal fulfilment, maximize your talents, and achieve your goals.

After these, your security and that of your most important resources is paramount, and you should also deploy your energy in ensuring this. If body and means are both safe and secure, then the right frame of mind can be achieved to plan the path forward. Therefore, the Junglepreneur should always takes steps necessary for safety, which starts with the consciousness of "safety first." The next step is to identify ways of keeping safe through techniques and systems that are available with personal application or by working with others who are skilled in this area.

Regular communications is the next most important rule for using your energy, as the ability to transmit simple and complex information using various media is critical to the survival and success of the Junglepreneur. No matter the situation, you really must always find a way to reach people and deploy your energy in this direction.

Once regular communication is achieved, the Junglepreneur has the critical capacity to pass on important messages and really get things done. When the Junglepreneur is operating in a new and unfamiliar location, one of the first things that must be done is to find a reliable means to communicate constantly. The military is aware of this great importance of communications. For them, it is the lifeblood of all military operations, and they do not play around with it. In a similar manner, the Junglepreneur must appreciate and protect communication ability by all means and at all costs. If the Junglepreneur has to choose between using resources for other things or using them to get communications, the choice for communications should be a high priority.

Communications for Emerging Markets: One example of what communications can achieve is a company based in Mexico called Frogtek, which is using mobile communications devices to empower small business owners. Frogtek developed innovative business tools hosted in a cloud environment specifically for the large number of shop owners in emerging countries like Colombia and Mexico. The simplified tool enables the shop owners to use scanners to manage their stock and sales with communications devices like mobile phones and tablets, through which they upload data to Frogtek's cloud environment. Without these mobile communications devices, the shop owners in these countries could not have accessed such cutting-edge solutions designed just for them.[10]

So with many important things to use your energy for, generating and preserving it should be a priority. This is so that you can effectively use your energy for all those things that really matter to your life, your business, and the society.

Chapter Six Takeaway: Energy Pointers

- Take control of your own energy by generating, protecting, and deploying it mainly toward succeeding in your terrain.
- Start your day with energizing positive thoughts and affirming statements from the second you open your eyes. Be free from negativity when you wake up so you start the day energized.
- Boost your energy in the morning with exercise, deep breathing, breakfast, and drinking water.
- Maintain and replenish your energy through the day by watching your thoughts, feeding, hydration, and breathing to ensure they are in line with good standards set in the morning.
- Avoid energy killers, or E-Killers, arising from situations or even relationships that can drain your energy and leave you tired, lethargic, and unproductive.
- Recognize manipulation, and limit being manipulated so it does not deplete your precious energy.
- Allocate some time out of the first eight hours in the day to work on your goals, and maximize the undissipated energy you get from this quiet time for more productivity.
- Understand business herd behavior so you gain from the synergy without wasting your own energy.
- Have backup plans up to Plan Z to avoid losing energy due to correcting things that go wrong.
- Use your saved energy to create value in the form of goods, services, inventions, or knowledge. Ensure mobility of all these and yourself.
- Deploy your preserved energy in networking effectively, to connect with loved ones, for achieving your personal goals, to communicate, and to secure your assets.

Seven
Knowledge for Managing Your Terrain

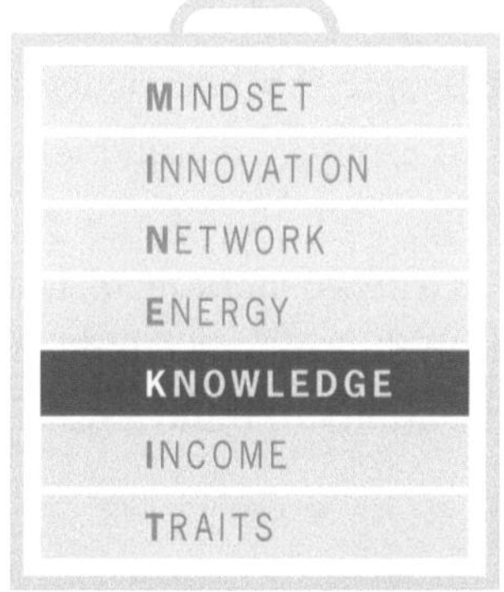

We make the world we live in and shape our own environment.
—Orison Swett Marden, acclaimed author of *Pushing to the Front*

Our ultimate freedom is the right and power to decide how anybody or anything outside ourselves will affect us.
—Stephen Covey, author of *7 Habits of Highly Effective People*

Business terrains are different in nature, with varied amounts of resources, opportunities, obstacles, and challenges. However, there are specific knowledge principles that are applicable and adaptable for managing most terrains to different degrees. This is the *K* in the Junglepreneur MINEKIT, and this knowledge for managing your terrains revolves around mainly three key points. These three are knowledge for managing your people, knowledge for devising your strategy, and knowledge for designing your systems. There are a host of other knowledge-based functionalities that will be considered in this chapter, but these first three are paramount; we will start from there.

People Knowledge

Theodore "Teddy" Roosevelt was sworn in as 26th American president at the age of 42 and became one of the youngest ever to date. He served between 1901 and 1909 and won a Nobel Peace Prize during his term. Roosevelt was successful in his career mainly because he had a great personality and was brilliant at relating to people. He is noted as saying that the most important ingredient in the formula of success is to know how to get along with people. So knowledge about how to manage people is therefore a most essential requirement for success. However, people are complex beings, and finding out all that is required to be successful with people is a huge amount of information. Three main skills, however, are critical: the ability to understand people, the ability to relate to them, and the ability to build a team. We will now consider all these in detail.

Understand People

Showing genuine interest in people and understanding them is vital to success, as the world and its affairs are all about people. Understanding people is also vital to interacting with them, but this may be easier said than done. Though people are an important resource, they are also the most intricate, unpredictable, and unknowable species in existence. It is very difficult to know what is really going on in the minds and hearts of people. Yet to be able to interact well and conduct business successfully, you need to have an idea of what people are likely to do or how they perceive you.

In understanding people, knowing the ways in which humans communicate is crucial. All animals or creatures use verbal and nonverbal communication either consciously or unconsciously, and humans are no different.[1] It is important to know that thought patterns from the brain are mirrored through the physical body in one form or another. Even though human beings may try to mask their true thoughts—and some are actually extremely good at this—there are still ways in which body language will reveal the true nature of the thoughts.

It is said that over 80 percent of communication by people is actually nonverbal, communicated through the body in the form of what are called *tells*.[2] Tells are movements that give away a particular indication of what exactly is going on in a person's mind. The eyelids, posture, lips, pupils, speech, hands, voice, and tone can all be read in a particular way to get exact messages from a person. Interpreting tells is a useful skill in understanding cues from other people and those that you give off yourself, all of which are very vital to business success.

Relate to People

Handling people successfully also involves a great deal of work on the part of the Junglepreneur. People skills are all about how one behaves with people, what is said, and how it is done. A person is made up of the visible part and invisible part. The visible part is the physical body and how it communicates with others. The invisible part includes thoughts, emotions, feelings, and attitudes, which cannot be seen and can only be guessed. Therefore, the most important aspect with regard to people skills is the actual behavior of the Junglepreneur, which is what determines how others see you and relate with you.

In the behavior of the Junglepreneur to others, it is important not to come across as defensive, aggressive, unfeeling, critical, arrogant, or lackadaisical. Use your body, voice, facial expressions, and movements in the proper manner to convey the right character. You want to come across as relaxed, open, friendly, supportive, assured, accommodating, and successful. It goes without saying that the behavior of others can also fall into the categories just described. It is important for the Junglepreneur to also work toward understanding and managing the behavior of other people. In doing this the behavioral patterns of other people must be carefully studied to see if they are the desired patterns. If they are, then all is well, but if they are not, try to redirect to the desired behavior by managing your emotions and those of others until you are close to your desired behavioral objective. Under no circumstances, though, should the Junglepreneur allow the behavior of others to derail the overall business vision.

Build Teams

Having the right team of people with the right mix of knowledge, skills, and talents is vital to the Junglepreneur. In conducting business, the Junglepreneur will need others' skills and resources to assist in the vision. It is extremely difficult to succeed in the jungle of the business world entirely alone. Very few people of immense success have ever done it by themselves. The Junglepreneur's team can include peers, friends, mentors, talented workers, family members—anyone with specialized abilities necessary for your business or even simply people to support you and help you grow. In essence a team needs to be built to maximize the combined power of a unified group of people toward achieving a common goal. Effective team-building has its foundations in the management theories of motivation.[3] However, effective team-building is also a practical skill that the Junglepreneur must constantly hone. It involves the following steps:

- Select the team members carefully, based on the specific skills and knowledge they possess, which are particularly suited to the goal or task ahead.
- Articulate the vision or goal for which the team is being built, and preferably do so in written form. The vision or goal must be realistic but challenging enough to justify putting a team in place to tackle it.
- Communicate this vision to the team and ensure that they understand it, that they know the purpose of the team, and that they also appreciate being a part of something larger than themselves.
- Establish and empower a leadership structure for the team, but set clear boundaries for engagement, which will be adhered to by the team leader. Clear operational guidelines for the team also need to be properly communicated.

- Ensure that team cohesion is established early and continuously during the project. The team becomes cohesive and collaborative through interpersonal understanding and cooperation among the team members.
- Build cohesion through team exercises that involve the team working together on light-hearted tasks which are separate from the vision from time to time. For instance, take the team out to a recreation center for some bonding pickup games, and watch how trust and closeness develop.
- Understand the needs of the team as a whole and the needs of the individual members. This is achieved by studying the team dynamics, personalities of the members, and personal interactions.
- Stimulate the team into innovation and creative thinking through exercises like brainstorming and mind mapping.
- Motivate the team by giving a clear picture of the corporate and personal rewards they stand to receive for achieving the overall vision. In this regard the team should be constantly encouraged by also celebrating important milestones attained toward the overall goal.
- Finally, review and document all the challenges and successes of the team at the end of the task. This can be used to establish a learning curve from which your future projects and teams can gain.

A great example of the power of building a team is Google, started by Sergei Brin and Larry Page in a Stanford dormitory.[4] The two founders of Google initially laid out the framework for the company and later brought in Eric Schmidt to join them in forming the core start-up team. Each of them had specific skills that they brought to the team, and for a while both Sergei Brin and Larry Page were co-founders in charge of technology and product development, while Eric Schmidt was CEO with operational responsibilities. Recently, Page has taken over as CEO, Schmidt is the Chairman with external partnership tasks, and Brin is responsible for special projects. Though they have been in different roles at various points, this core team has remained since inception, and with persistent focus, they have built Google into the world's largest internet search engine and a technology giant.

In contrast to Google's small core, the John Lewis Partnership in the UK is one of the world's largest business teams, with almost 85,000 members. John Lewis, one of the most successful retailers in the UK, with revenue of over nine billion pounds sterling, was founded by the company's namesake in 1864. It was his son and successor, John Spedan Lewis, who in 1909, while recovering from a riding accident, developed a unique idea to form the employees of John Lewis into one large motivated stakeholder team.

The John Lewis Team: Spedan Lewis went on to establish the John Lewis Partnership in 1929 through a trust deed and spelled out the group's vision clearly in this quote: "The partnership's ultimate purpose is the happiness of all its members through their worthwhile and satisfying employment in a successful business."[5] The partnership sees the employees as part of one large team who all have a stake in the business and share in its profits. At John Lewis, the partnership, which also has a membership council, ensures employees earn an extra 10 to 20 percent of their salaries as a bonus from the profits of the firm. The partners have superb leisure facilities, get to elect almost half of the directors, and also have a say in the management decisions.

It is important to note that the team members do not necessarily have to work for you, know you intimately, or even physically be around you as long as you have access to them or their resources when you need them. In some cases, the Junglepreneur may have to compensate the required people to get them on the team. One way or another, time needs to be spent carefully identifying the people needed and finding ways to motivate or gain access to them. If the Junglepreneur does have a team of people that works for the project, it is vital to also invest in the team's training and development and keep it well compensated.

As part of the team, there will be some few key people who are always there for the Junglepreneur, are most supportive, and are willing to go the extra mile without any ulterior motive or compensation in mind. Such people are rare to have, and one must be willing to reciprocate their support. If one is lucky enough to have them, then there is a principle that the Junglepreneur must apply to this set of people. It is called *giri*. [6]

> In Japanese, *giri* connotes a 'give and give' relationship. It requires that you must be fiercely loyal and be there for people who have supported you even if it will be costly or will be inconvenient to you.[7]

For the people who have supported the Junglepreneur, there must be no excuses when reciprocity is required, as it is *giri* that the Junglepreneur be there for them when needed.

Strategy Knowledge

We now move on to our next knowledge key point: strategy. Author and known strategist William E. Rothschild commented concerning strategy, "What do you want to achieve or avoid? The answers to this question are objectives. How will you go about achieving your desired results? The answer to this you can call strategy." Strategy is one of the knowledge keystones to business survival and is a specialized plan or roadmap toward success. Strategy means considering the external environment of the Junglepreneur, including its opportunities and threats. It also means taking into consideration the internal environment of the business, its strengths and weaknesses, and the strengths and weaknesses of the Junglepreneur and the team. Strategy also involves the decisions of the Junglepreneur and how to contain and maximize the internal and external environments. Your strategy details what needs to be done, how to do it, when to do it, and what resources will be required. It should be laid out with an action plan specifically designed for your unique terrain. Your strategy is best kept simple and practical, with clear action points for how you are going to achieve it.

Strategy also involves a great deal of forecasting for future occurrences that may affect the business and recognizing the options for managing the issues that may arise. This will involve a thorough assessment of the goals and objectives for the business terrain, an audit of the resources in the terrain, and a final plan for how to maximize the opportunities. The final plan will include a system for implementation, monitoring, assessing, and measuring the performance of the plans against the identified goals and objectives for the business terrain. The Junglepreneur's strategy should also include considerations for how to attract and retain customers. This could be a low-cost-entry strategy or a differentiation strategy for products or services. Strategic plans can also include divestment strategies, business-growth estimations, and market-share development strategies.

Seconds Count: When the Nigerian government started granting mobile-phone licenses in the 2001, the first two authorized phone providers had the first-mover strategic advantage and billed customers on a per-minute billing system. Then two years later, Mike Adenuga's Globacom was also granted a license but faced an uphill task in winning market share. Adenuga and his team strategized and researched into what the market really wanted. With the knowledge gained by strategic market research, they realized consumers in this emerging market really desired a per-second billing system, as it was much cheaper for them to manage their calls. So Globacom pushed for a per-second billing system with the regulatory bodies and pioneered it in the market.[8] Through this strategic move, they won massive market share and subsequently increased their subscriber base to about twenty million subscribers.

So in the business jungle, the Junglepreneur strategy must also include a series of steps and mechanisms that will help with survival when in a tight spot. Remember that the golden rule for the business jungle is survival, so the survival of your business is paramount. Antelopes in the jungle love the fresh grass on the open fields, but if they are not constantly aware of the principle of survival, they will only make nice meals for the cheetahs hiding in the bushes.

Systems Knowledge

Systems are methods used to manage resources and which have the direct responsibility for converting resource inputs into vital goods and services required to engage in successful business. Michael Gerber, author of *E-Myth Revisited*, argues for the building of systems within every business function and allowing the systems to run the business while the people then run the systems.[9] The knowledge about building systems is therefore foundational or peripheral, depending on the business terrain or objective. There are different types of systems, including sales systems, production systems, transport and logistics systems, financial systems, and human-management systems.

Systems in themselves have their own internal processes that define the mode, pattern, rate, and level of activity and delivery. Processes in one system also link to other processes in the different systems to form one cohesive network of functionalities that make a business succeed. John Jantsch, author of *Duct Tape Marketing*, says that every functioning business is primarily a set of systems and processes.[10] So the ability to recognize and manage the exact systems and processes required to make a business successful is a useful skill set.

Lean Toyota: The very successful Toyota lean production system gives an avid reference to the importance of processes and systems. Developed by Toyota engineers and management between 1950 and 1980, the system revolves around a *just-in-time* production principle, which seeks to eliminate waste of time, stock, movement, and processing.[11] The system also seeks to achieve a continuous flow in processes by identifying the root causes of various problems, avoiding overproduction, and preventing system overload. The Toyota production system also empowers its processes through a workplace philosophy of continuous improvement in operations, teamwork, personal reflection, and respect for people. Toyota gained knowledge about systems to build an effective production system that has worked excellently for the organization.

There are additional areas in which having knowledge will be useful for managing your terrain successfully. Let us move on to these.

Time Management

English author and playwright Arnold Bennet once said, "The supply of time is a daily miracle. You wake up in the morning and lo! Your purse is magnificently filled with 24 hours of the unmanufactured tissue of the universe of life. It is yours! The most precious of your possessions."[12] Time as it is known to us consists of 24 hours (or 1,440 minutes, or 86,400 seconds, depending on how you choose to look at it) that make up one single day. In a single week there are 168 hours. It is often said that to make a significant impact regarding any vision, there must be a consistent commitment of about 60 to 70 percent out of the total hours available every week. Into this space of 168 hours a week, we also squeeze in time for all of life's essential activities. The ability to manage all the activities that need to be done in the given space of time is the real meaning of time management. In reality, managing time itself is not possible, since time cannot be controlled. Therefore the focus of managing time should be on the activities we use time for. So to utilize time well, it is important for the Junglepreneur to be a self-starter who is not reactive to situations as they arise. The Junglepreneur must specifically carve up every minute and hour of time to know exactly what it will be spent on. Concerning this proper use of time, Ted W. Engstrom, former head of a very large humanitarian aid organization called World Vision International, advises that one should ask the following questions: "What do you want to get done? In what order of importance? Over what period of time? What is the time available? What is the best strategy for application of time to projects for the most effective results?" In this regard it will be useful to also encourage simplicity in conducting business to save useful time. This is except in cases where there is a real need for extensive and time-consuming detail that can be justified in relation to valuable contributions it will make toward achieving your goal.

The Junglepreneur's Time Value of Time

You have 24 hours in any given day to accomplish your goals. Since the past is the past and you only have the present and future time, therefore I argue that just like the value of money can be different in the present versus the future—known as the time value of money—similarly over the present and future time, the time value of time is also higher. Therefore the value of the present time which one has and the future time to come is very valuable. So I call this the Junglepreneur's *Time Value of Time*, which is how the businessperson in a tough terrain recognizes the power of what can be done now in the present time and also the great things that can be achieved in the future time to come. It is then very important to use the present time effectively and plan well too for the use of the future time even before it arrives. A useful exercise is to prepare an hour-by-hour schedule for how every hour will be spent and then keep a daily record of actual activities. This will show you how much time you are spending on certain activities and if the time cycle can be reduced by faster or more efficient action. Determine to always control your own agenda and the demands made on your time by deciding very early each day which activities will take priority for that day. A useful way of doing this is to categorize demands on your time into the following:

- Pressing and important,
- Pressing but not important,
- Important but not pressing, and
- Not pressing and not important.

After this categorization, start with focusing your time on those activities which require your immediate attention and are also very important. Then going forward you can spend your time on issues according to their order of importance as you determine it. Trying to achieve this may also require you to delay in attending to some situations to buy time for more important activities. In some cases it may even require you to politely refuse some demanding time commitments that do not fit into your plan for the day. It may also be necessary to apply this technique to all time-consuming activities, including meetings, visits, phone calls, emails, social networking, or any activity that will use up your time, no matter how small the time demand is. If you are able to, you could also delegate non-priority tasks to free up more time. It is also important to watch out for time-devouring activities like too much leisure time, which could eat away at the productive minutes of the day. As Phillip Stranhope, the British statesman best known as Lord Chesterfield, once noted, "If one learns to take care of the minutes, the hours will take care of themselves."[13]

There is also the phenomenon called *dead time*, which arises from time spent on activities that directly prevent you from other tasks. Commuting and household chores are the most common examples of this. Dead time can still be put to good use by incorporating some mind exercises like deep thinking, arithmetic, composing future correspondence, or practicing spelling. You can also use this time to listen to personal development tapes or audio books.

Generally a good variety of activities is important to ensure a well-balanced lifestyle and a successful business. William Frederick Book, a professor emeritus of psychology at Indiana University until he passed away in 1940, said of time that "a man must be master of his hours and days, not their servant." In doing this, you should constantly focus your productive time on your main goals and vision. Then continually measure your time-dependent activities in relation to how much they have contributed to your goals over a particular time span.

Handling Complexity

Most tough business environments are in a constant state of complexity, chaos, and change. An ever-moving vortex of activity that, like a tornado, may suck the Junglepreneur in if he or she does not know how to handle rapid change. Complexity and turbulence are the order of the day in the business jungle—in fact they are the very essence of it—whereby you have a myriad number of situations, opportunities, issues, and tasks all demanding immediate attention. Complexity goes hand in hand with rapid change and requires different skill sets and mental capacity. Flexibility and adaptability are major keys to handling complexity and change, as they enable one to blend with every situation as it presents itself and achieve successful results. Important skills for dealing with complexity are also the ability to decompile the complex into the simple and the ability to multitask by carrying out different tasks at the same time. Multitasking also enables us to roam the power of our mind from one activity to another and make multiple decisions all in a continuous fashion.

In relation to managing complexity by the process of decompiling, it is useful to note that you can accomplish any complex task as long as you can break it down into small enough pieces.

Eating Planes: Michel Lotito, a French-born entertainer, became world-renowned for his ability to eat items like metal, plastics, or glass that are not normally consumable by humans. Between 1978 and 1980, Lotito actually ate a whole Cessna 150 airplane by breaking it into very small pieces and consuming gradually over the space of two years. He did this by carving out about 1kg (about 2 ¼ lbs.) from the plane every day and breaking the chunk down into small chip-sized pieces. He would consume mineral oil first to lubricate his throat and gullet and help with swallowing. He then started eating the chip-sized parts of the plane and drinking plenty of water as he ate. He did this consistently every day for two years until the whole plane was consumed.[14]

Though eating a plane is an extreme example, which I would not advise you to try, it does depict how you can learn to come to grips with complex situations. This involves first breaking down the components to their very simplest form and then assimilating the necessary tasks required to accomplish the goal.

Maximizing Opportunities

In the business sense, opportunities are the rearrangement of circumstances to present an opening to add or gain value. Opportunities are also the potential ability to accomplish beyond the set targets of a goal or objective. A significant wave of opportunity may come only once or twice in every person's life, and if ridden well, it can take him or her to shores of success unimagined. For the Junglepreneur it is critical to be able to identify and maximize opportunities. US Senator Robert F. Kennedy was quoted as saying, "All of us might wish at times that we lived in a more tranquil world, but we don't. And if our times are difficult and perplexing, so are they challenging and filled with opportunity."[15]

In identifying opportunities, a useful exercise would be to compare ideal life or business situations to the actual situation of life in your terrain and note the gaps. These gaps are possible opportunities to provide a product or service. Recognizing the opportunity also involves carefully considering the nature of circumstances and the potential they have to generate value. Once the situation or circumstance has this potential to generate reasonable value, then it is likely to be an opportunity.

Against the Odds: A case to consider is that of Sung-Joo Kim, a South Korean lady who has had remarkable success in her terrain.[16] Sung-Joo was from a wealthy family but decided on her own to go to the United States to study further, against the wishes of her family, which were for her to marry into another wealthy family. It was challenging to remain in school in America without the financial support of her family, and to fend for herself, she went to work for Bloomingdale's stores. There she had the opportunity to learn about the fashion industry in great detail. With time she gained experience and contacts, and she then spotted a major opportunity in a German brand called MCM. The MCM brand was in decline at that time due to management issues, but Sung-Joo was convinced that the brand was still strong and could generate value. She also recognized that it had an opportunity in South Korea. So she raised funds and bought over the MCM brand in 2005, and she has gone on to actually build it into a very successful fashion company in Korea, which also licensed leading brands into that market.

For Sung-Joo, this was her own significant wave of opportunity. All the circumstances necessary to crystallize it were in place, but she first had to recognize the opportunity and then influence the process by deploying resources and taking action. She has gone on to ride the opportunity well, to the maximum benefit of herself, her 600 employees in South Korea, her customers, and the larger society.[17]

Risk Knowledge

The Junglepreneur must develop the capacity to identify and recognize any potential business risk. This is especially critical in harsh or unstable business conditions, which may have a higher level of embedded risk. It is important to know, however, that where there are high risks there are also high rewards. It all depends on the Junglepreneur's risk appetite, or capacity to handle risk. In most cases, younger people have a higher risk appetite, as there is time left to recover, while older people are more risk-averse, as they may have limited recovery opportunities. However, this is not a strict rule and can be personality-dependent, since a person may be young and have no appetite for risk at all or vice versa.

The Junglepreneur should, however, be willing to embrace reasonable risk, as risk is to the Junglepreneur what dumbbells are to a bodybuilder. Just as lifting enough weights challenges your body and helps your muscles grow, in the same way, embracing risk helps the Junglepreneur to develop capacity and strength for the difficult road ahead. We all have different growth capacities and risk appetites, so the Junglepreneur should not become envious or discouraged by others' success. Calculated and well-informed risk-taking can be very rewarding to the Junglepreneur, but excessive risk should be avoided, as it is closer to gambling and can result in devastating losses.

Additionally, once you feel any warning bells, you should reconsider taking action, as the key is to survive and have another opportunity in future to do better and more profitable business. You must not worry and think that whatever very risky opportunity is before you is the only meal ticket for the foreseeable future. It is not, and somehow you will find a way to live until the next opportunity.

Risk

The Junglepreneur must also learn to identify different kinds of risk—political, financial, environmental, and others—and make plans to manage them. Tough terrains are very risky environments, and so risk is quite central to the Junglepreneur's surviving and thriving. Therefore, let us go deeper into the concept of risk, risk classes, and risk management. The word *risk* itself originated around 1830 from the French word *risqué* and is defined as "those set of opportunities for which you cannot guarantee the returns."[18] Risk is also the possibility that a damaging occurrence could lead to a loss or conversely that a favorable occurrence could lead to gains. Risk can be categorized in three categories based on the amount of information available. Former US Secretary of Defense Donald Rumsfeld's description of *known knowns, known unknowns,* and *unknown unknowns* can be used here to depict what constitutes risk in this context.[19]

The *unknown unknowns* are events with the highest unpredictable probability. Risk is linked to uncertainty, though the two concepts differ in that, while uncertainty comes from a scarcity of information, risk is embedded in the actual situation itself. The concept of risk entails that uncertainty must be present in the results of actions taken, as guaranteed outcomes mean the absence of risk. To differentiate between risk and uncertainty, there is a simple test you can carry out. When you don't know for sure exactly what will happen, but you know the odds or chances of occurrence, that is risk. However, if you don't even know the odds of anything happening at all, that is uncertainty.[20] So the importance of risk is derived from our lack of capacity to predict future events, and this now introduces the element of chance. The introduction of chance into the choice of possible outcomes forces the making of decisions under conditions of risk both personal and difficult, depending on individual responses to risk. In this regard risk and decision making are then further linked to human behavior and information. So making decisions in the presence of uncertainty requires comparing the possible positive benefits against the possible negative consequences. Therefore, making informed decisions that can tackle the issues around uncertainty relies greatly on how good your information is about your territory.[21]

Types and Classes of Risk

There are two types of risk, the first being *pure* or *downside risk*, which is described as the possibility that the outcome we expect is what we get or that something bad will happen and a total loss will occur. This type of risk, like the loss of an asset, can be mitigated with insurance policies. The second type of risk is *two-way* or *speculative risk* and happens when the outcome either could be better or worse than we expected. Tough business terrains naturally have speculative risk, as business or income expectations could be either higher or lower than expected.[22] Now the classification of risk is the identification of those prominent pure or speculative risks that can be encountered. The following are classes of risk:[23]

- Market risk occurs from a change in market events like the price of an asset or an interest rate.
- Liquidity risk is when cash outflow needs cannot be met by cash inflows.
- Credit risk results from the lack of performance of a firm that leads to a failure to come up with funds or securities when required.
- Legal risk may incur loss if a contract that was deemed enforceable proves not to be or when a litigation claim is made on the company.
- Intellectual risk occurs when human resources with specialized knowledge are no longer available or accessible.
- Business risks are related to regular business operations and comprised of product risks, risk of losing customers, macroeconomic risk from unanticipated economic situations, and technology risk arising from change in technology.[24]

Risk Management

Risk management concerns your selection of the kind and amount of risks that are acceptable for you to handle. Risk management can be also described as the actions that are carried out to avoid uncertainty and that allow you to identify, assess, and manage risks. Enterprise risk management, also known as integrated risk management, is an aspect of risk management that deals with a whole spectrum of comprehensive risks that can affect you, your business, the environment, resources, assets, etc. Being very inclusive, enterprise risk management deals with broad risk issues ranging from financial to operational to general business risk. So the whole process of risk management, including its enterprise aspect, is worth knowing and deploying in tough terrains. This risk-management process is outlined below:[25]

- Start by outlining your overall strategic objective goal or vision for which you need to manage risks that can affect it.
- Undertake risk assessment by identifying all the possible risk exposures to your vision or goal. Then estimate the level of these risk exposures and assess the possible effects of the exposures.
- Audit identified risk exposures by evaluating them for embedded opportunities and threats.
- Mitigate risk threats and opportunities by articulating your risk-mitigation strategy, which can used to increase opportunity risks and reduce threat risks.
- Conclude your risk-management process with the constant monitoring of already identified risks and also potential risks. This includes assessing the performance and the effectiveness of your risk-management process itself.[26]

Having discussed the concept of risk, it cannot be overemphasized that before carrying out any risk-involving activity, all efforts must be made to get as much substantiated information as possible. There is a place for trying to use your gut instinct in making decisions that involve risk. However, as we have identified, the element of risk that makes it so unusual is not knowing the odds of what can occur. So trying to reduce the level of uncertainty is a very important exercise in managing risk. Reducing uncertainty can be achieved by avoiding acting on unsubstantiated information or your personal feelings alone. It will rather be better to involve experienced professionals for advice and also monitor the environment for indicative time-tested signals. Doing these will bring out more facts, figures, and correct information, which can help to reduce the level of uncertainty. Therefore, you can base your decisions on what you can measure, rather than basing risky decisions on uncertainty fueled by lack of the right information.

We have just considered how to manage the tough business terrain, and this chapter combines with the previous ones as a foundation for the next chapter. In this next chapter we will look at the topic of how to make money in any business terrain.

Chapter Seven Takeaway: Junglepreneur Knowledge

- Acquire specific knowledge that is necessary for adapting to your business terrain and succeeding in it. The first three areas are knowledge about people, strategy, and systems.
- Learn how to manage human beings, as it is an essential requirement for your success in any terrain. You do this by understanding people, relating to them, and building teams.
- Get knowledge on strategy, which gives you a detailed plan for your success. It is a keystone for your business survival and for taming your terrain.
- Achieve understanding in the knowledge about the intricacies of business systems. Systems are mechanisms used to convert resource inputs into outputs in an efficient process, and they are vital to the Junglepreneur.
- Manage your time by managing well the activities your time is used for. Do this by carving up your daily time by the minute and hour, and then monitor and record how each unit of your time is spent.
- Get a grip on complexity and turbulence, which are characteristics of tough terrains. Achieve this by decompiling the complex into simple units. Also learn to multitask, and be flexible and adaptable to the terrain.
- Ensure you can identify your terrain opportunities efficiently. Do this by comparing the actual business situations to the desired in your terrain then noting the gaps that have the potential to generate reasonable value and be maximized.
- Identify potential business risks in your terrain and the level of risks you can handle. Manage the risks by assessing them, taking steps to reduce their uncertainty, and making plans to mitigate them.

Eight
Income in the Business Jungle

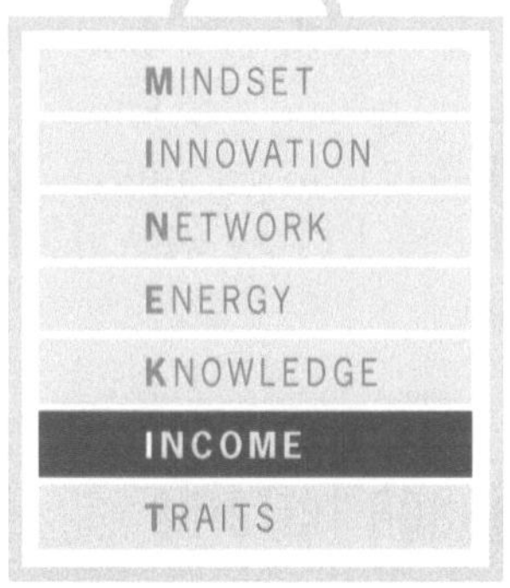

Wealth flows from energy and ideas.
—William Feather, American publisher

Making money is an art.
—Andy Warhol

In Junglepreneur MINEKIT, the second *I* is the income, or the value that you earn in your terrain, which goes a long way toward validating your efforts and sustaining you. Earning your income often involves money, which is essentially a means of exchange—a store of value for future use. Even in the toughest terrains, people who invest their time well make money every single day. There is an old African adage that says, "Food or money is in the mouth of the lion." The question is, who is brave enough to go and get it?

The Massai warriors of Africa have actually devised strategies for taking fresh meat away from lions. In this risky escapade, the Massai warriors start by walking shoulder to shoulder and moving forward in unison. They then begin to act in peculiar ways known only to them that actually scare wild, hungry lions away from their freshly killed prey. Incredibly, after scaring the lions off, the warriors then walk away with the meat in the full view of the lions.[1]

Taking food from the mouth of a lion really is possible to the person who has great courage and also know-how. That person is the Junglepreneur, who will decide to get a piece of the pie by doing all it takes to acquire it legally. So let's see what the Junglepreneur needs to do to make some money.

Making Money in Tough Terrains

Be assured that even in the dry desert there is money to be made. No matter how rough or tough the terrain is, one can make good money if the know-how is there. So how does one do this? First, there is money to be made all around, and it is closer than you think. One needs to take closer notice of things within the immediate vicinity to see opportunities just like Tony Fadell of NEST Labs took a closer look at a thermostat and built a successful company out of the experience. Let's now consider some important steps to making money in tough terrains.

Track the Money

Making money in a tough terrain can indeed be challenging, as such terrains may give the appearance of scarcity. However, even in the harshest of terrains, there is money moving around daily. So a good place to start is to track and follow where and how money flows in your terrain. Though one may or may not physically see the money, it is all around, but you have to follow it very closely. To track the money flow in your terrain, consider the following points.

Identify Local Income Streams

Start by finding out the biggest economic forces in your region that determine its income. The region's income stream is its revenue earned from one or a combination of the following: natural resources, licensing, commodities, taxes, tourism, technology, innovation, etc.[2] There may also be unreported incomes earned through the informal economy, which a few cities or nations may have and may not admit to. However, in most countries of the world, the sources are easily identifiable. You can also make it a habit of finding out the income stream of every city visited on business or holiday. However, start with the city where you conduct business.

There are usually a few streams of income that cities or countries primarily depend on to survive. They have worked this out over time, based on the resources and opportunities available to that location. Knowing the income stream of your city is important because this is the economic lifeline of that terrain. The income stream is like a river, and it is what drives all commerce; money flows into and money flows out of that region. The income source essentially drives all life and living in that city, and the Junglepreneur needs to be aware of the source and be connected to it.

Identify Big Spending Patterns

After knowing the income stream of the region, the next step is to identify when, how, and where the government and businesses spend their money. Governments and large corporations in most areas are the biggest spenders and employers, and it is important to know their spending patterns.[3] For instance, when are their budgets prepared? What is the average yearly size of their budgets? When and how are funds released, and who approves the spending?

Having identified the income streams, budget patterns, and spending priorities of the terrain, the Junglepreneur can then really start the process of making money by tapping into this flow. However, there is still a bit more to find out. You need to follow the money in relation to the people around you.

Ascertain People's Earning Patterns

Next you need to know how the majority of the people in your region earn their own income, when they earn it, and what they spend their money on. In doing this, it is important to identify the people's working profiles, needs, and wants. For instance, you can ascertain if the people in your terrain are mostly salaried workers who get their income at the end of the month or if they are businesspeople with flexible earning cycles. Then to know about their needs and wants, you can consider if people in your terrain spend their income on consumer goods, technology, or tourism, or if in your terrain they rather spend their income on providing their own private services like personal power-generators, water, health, etc. It could even be that you notice that the spending priorities in your terrain are on such things as education, research, and development. Spending varies from city to city and country to country, and you need to be aware of what goes on in your terrain of operation. Having this information helps you to know what goods and services will sell in your territory and when the purchases are likely to be made.

Know the Marketplace

It is advisable for the Junglepreneur to visit the marketplaces in the terrain to closely observe what is going on and directly interact with the people involved. Marketplaces are anywhere where the business and trade governance of the terrain is being conducted. Marketplaces could be on the internet or in physical spaces such as local markets, technology clusters, shopping malls, business districts, large office complexes, city centers, etc. Visiting the online and physical marketplaces enables one to have a feel of what the businesses in that terrain are all about. It gives the Junglepreneur a finger on the pulse of commerce for that terrain. Interacting directly with the marketplace lets you know what goods or services are being traded, how and when they are traded, and also who the people involved are.

Build Junglepreneur Money Pipes

After acquiring all the information discussed above, you need to find your own niche through a service or product you will provide in exchange for money. You need to devise a legal way to create your own Junglepreneur Money Pipes to this money flow, which will allow a constant stream of income to flow in your direction.

> Junglepreneur Money Pipes are constructed by creating systems for efficiently producing and delivering your product(s) or service(s) of good value at the least cost to the largest number of customers possible who really need it on a regular basis and who will flow back regular payments to you in exchange.

Through desire, belief, focus, providence, and effort, the Junglepreneur decides how large the flow in the money pipes will be. The larger you can make it, the more money flows to you. Junglepreneur Money Pipes can be created in any of the following areas: trading, manufacturing, professional services, construction, communications, transportation, etc. The important thing is to start the process and grow from there until you are strong enough to step the business up. However, to do this you first need to know the skills you have that can help with the construction of the pipes.

Do a Skills and Opportunities Audit

To build Junglepreneur Money Pipes to connect to the money flows, an important exercise to carry out is a skills and opportunities audit. You will need to sit down and carefully think through all the skills and opportunities that you have. You could also ask someone close to you to help with this process, as they would see you objectively. The goal is to identify those personal skills and attributes you possess that mark you out as distinct and excellent.[4] Next also identify all your opportunities, but then focus on the very few that have good earning potential and that you would do well at and enjoy. The great poet Maya Angelou said, "You can only become truly accomplished at something you love. Don't make money your goal. Instead, pursue the opportunities that you love doing, and then do them so well that people can't take their eyes off you."[5] Now once the Junglepreneur can identify those things that are loved, then doing these should be the main goals that are executed, and the money will flow toward him or her.

So now with all the strength, focus, and courage you can muster, begin to apply those very few particular skills, talents, and abilities that you really excel in toward constructing your Junglepreneur Money Pipes in the areas you love and enjoy. You can also find others who can contribute their skills to help your vision as well. If the Junglepreneur is able to do all these, earning good income even in tough terrains will be a rewarding and enriching experience.

Hunt for the Junglepreneur's Big Game

Walt Disney, founder of the company that bears his name, postulated that you have the capacity to do anything you can dream about. At some point in your moneymaking adventure, you will need to hunt for your own big game. Big game in the jungle parlance are large animals that are hunted based on their size, like buffalos, bison, and king deer.[6] Make no mistake, big game can be tricky to hunt, and the predator attempting big game does so at some level of risk. However, many predators do it all the same and most times succeed. In the business jungle, it is not much different.

> Big game can be likened to having a very big vision, structuring large business transactions, executing immense projects, or building a colossal business and financial "engine" that generates large and consistent cash flow and income.

When Gordon Selfridge founded Selfridges exclusive shops in London in 1909, he went for big game by having the dream of his shops stretching all the way from Oxford Street up to Wigmore Street with a dome larger than that of the St. Paul's Cathedral.[7] Today even though Selfridges stores have passed on to other owners, the dream still lives on.

Selfridges has a massive store in London, and others in Manchester and Birmingham, with total floor space of over 500,000 square feet.

The people who succeed at the highest level in business, even in tough terrains, make it a point of duty to go for big game regularly. Before going for big game, the Junglepreneur will need to build up some knowledge, confidence, and experience first. Then, when the opportunity presents itself, the Junglepreneur must attempt to go for and get big game. It is worth it, as the experience is not only educational, exhilarating, and extremely rewarding, but it is also a great confidence booster and reputation enhancer for even greater success. Here are some more pointers for hunting your Junglepreneur big game in your business terrain:

- Have big goals, ideas, and targets.
- Target big game at least once in your career, as it is easier to catch than you think, and it feeds you longer.
- Use the power of teamwork to help you snag the biggest game.
- Put in your effort for big game, as it is almost the same effort required for small game too.

So at the right time conduct your risk assessment, and if you get good signals, hunt your big game and go for it without any fear or trepidation.

Have Good Cash Flow

Understanding the importance of cash flow is vital to making money. Money as a store of value exists in various forms, but the most popular is in the form of physical cash. Since cash is vital, getting and giving resources to a business is critical. The survival of your business depends a great deal on how you are able to keep cash constantly moving in and out of the business system through its expenses and earnings. This is what is referred to as cash flow, or liquidity, and you must maintain this by all legal means to avoid your business systems grinding to a halt.

A business may have money stored in other forms besides currency, though, such as physical buildings, bonds, shares, or commodities. However, some of these assets may not be easily convertible to cash at the immediate time required. So a company can have solid assets and yet still be insolvent, meaning it has no cash to meet its immediate obligations. When this happens everything freezes up in that business, and nothing can be done. So it is very important that a business has liquidity to enable it to keep transacting. Maintaining cash flow is a skilled balancing act of monitoring the amount of cash that comes in and that goes out of a business at specific times to ensure the business stays afloat. It is a skilled task that requires a skillful hand. Even if the Junglepreneur gets someone to handle this for the business, it is still something the Junglepreneur must learn personally so as to have a finger on the pulse of the business at all times. Managing your cash flow will involve preparing realistic budgets, projecting income and expenditures, managing invoices and payments, and keeping a close eye on the patterns of money movement within the business.

Deploy the Junglepreneur Bread-and-Butter Strategy

Since good cash flow is so critical to making money and survival, having a strategy that can help with this for short cycles will be useful at some point in your journey. The strategy is to make sure you have a business or an aspect of the intended business that directly generates cash very regularly or is vitally connected to another business that does. The aim of this strategy is to give the Junglepreneur decent short-cycle cash flows as a guarantee for business and personal survival while growing and targeting the big game.

> The Junglepreneur bread-and-butter strategy involves setting up small- and medium-scale businesses that have to do with direct cash payments by customers. The transportation, food, beverage, retail, consumer, education, and mobile-phone sectors offer many opportunities here. This is why it is called a bread-and-butter strategy, since the regular cash income after expenses keeps food on the table and also keeps your business running daily.

The Junglepreneur bread-and-butter strategy helps as a survival fall-back plan for tough times or when big business is slow. Through it you can generate survival income and even increase it by widening and deepening your customer base by creating more products and services. The strategy will help you keep things going for a while until you get out of tough times or business improves.

Build Reputation

Before I proceed with the rest of this chapter, it is important to discuss the aspect of reputation, since to make money, the Junglepreneur will need a solid and dependable reputation. Reputation often precedes one and is what that person is known for in the world. It is a combination of character, personality, abilities, skills, prowess, intellect, track record, and achievements. It is best if the Junglepreneur has a generally good reputation and is known for being an expert who possesses specialist skills in a particular field. Huge rewards will come from this. Making money in your terrain will also rely a great deal on reputation.

Regarding reputation, there was once a fellow who in high school had a hobby of picking the pockets of his friends without their knowing. He always returned the items lifted, since he was not really a thief. He just did it for laughs and because he could. However, his friends soon started calling him by the nickname *Crooked* for his thieving abilities. Even though he was actually a decent guy, the name *Crooked* caught on around his school. Many years later, he became a budding banker, and his old friends had a hard time reconciling his old nickname of *Crooked* with a high-trust career like banking. Needless to say his old friends were not among his first customers. The Junglepreneur must work on building and maintain a good reputation early and often, as your reputation can last for years even if you have undergone a complete character change.

Get Capital

Capital for business cannot be gained without first having a good reputation. Having just discussed the importance of reputation, we can move now into looking more closely at capital. Capital is the value or resources required as investment to start and grow a business. Capital is very important to every business, so the Junglepreneur must learn how to source it and how to maintain it. However, note that the most important capital that a Junglepreneur can have is his own person.

The greatest capital is inside of you and in you. Wayne Dyer, the renowned motivational speaker, said "Successful people attract money. They bring success to what they do." Therefore, people will throw money and resources at the person who knows which direction to go, what to do, and how and when to do it in the pursuit of business. Great fortunes have been built by people who started with virtually nothing but went on to attract all that they needed. The person with nothing but a great mind, confidence, purpose, and strong beliefs will attract all that is required to conduct any business affairs. The Junglepreneur is this kind of person.

Cash Capital

Cash capital is money in the form of actual cash that is invested in a business as capital. It is one of the most preferred forms of investment, as cash is a powerful form of capital to get a business started. Cash capital if not personally owned can also be attracted from banks or financial institutions, venture capitalists, angel investors, family, friends, government, or charitable organizations. The key to attracting cash capital from any investment source is investor confidence that the Junglepreneur has a viable venture with foreseeable profit and acceptable turnaround time. This is in addition to a good operating plan, a sound and reasonable financial plan, a likeable and trustworthy personality, and the personal drive to see the project through. The Junglepreneur may not have all these qualities alone, but she can put together a team that has all that is required.

However, the Junglepreneur who lacks any of the vital skills and qualities should start working hard at personal improvement first before forming a team. If the Junglepreneur does not work on all-around development but simply looks for a team member to fill this role, then the Junglepreneur will always be lacking in that area. The Junglepreneur need not be an expert in everything but should always have good foundational knowledge of the field. After building up a basic foundation, the Junglepreneur can then find others who have the qualities or skills required. The team will then be a great complement to what the Junglepreneur is already familiar with. This will make the Junglepreneur and the team more cohesive and effective toward achieving the business objective.

Now, cash alone does not have the sole preference as capital, and some new ventures have even been known to start without any initial cash. Success in business, projects, or transactions requires other forms, like asset capital or sweat capital, and we will now consider these other forms.

Asset Capital

Another form of capital is asset capital, which is resources in the form of physical assets like property, vehicles, shares, material inputs, bonds, inventory, plants and machinery, and intellectual property. Investors may decide to commit assets, which are given a specific value and brought in as a form of capital. The Junglepreneur should note that the assets required need not be expensive or even of very high value. You might be amazed at the level of business success that can be achieved by starting with just a laptop or smartphone or simply working from a kitchen table or garage. Very many large firms of today, including many Fortune 500 tech companies in America, started out from the garage of one of the founders. They probably did not care to consider what the neighbors or other people would think about their starting location, but rather they focused on the future of the business. Multi-billion dollar companies like Apple, Google, Amazon, and Hewlett-Packard all started from one home garage or another. Those garages are now historical business landmarks, so never underestimate what you have as an asset. It could just be the seed required for the making of a great company. What really matters is the mindset and focus of the Junglepreneur at that point in time.

Sweat Capital

Sweat capital is another form of capital, whereby an investor without access to cash or property may offer to do a certain amount of the physical and intellectual work required for a business or project. This also has great importance, and a value can be assigned to the sweat capital as a form of investment in the project. For budding businesspeople without cash and assets or businessmen with a lot of experience, this is a preferred route to become investors or part-owners in businesses. Quite a number of the technology multi-millionaires started out with sweat capital in exchange for a share of the business. They then worked very hard, doing most of the physical and intellectual work required to make it a success, and later on they reaped immense value from their appreciated shares.

For you this should always be a preferred route, even if you have assets or cash to invest. The route of sweat capital teaches the values of delayed gratification and willingness to initially work for nothing. Those who are able to master the great values of delayed gratification early or at some crucial point in life will always be set apart for success. Investing sweat capital will also give you an opportunity to stretch once again while working on a project, and you will come away from the experience much improved as a businessperson.

Harold S. Geneen, the former CEO and Chairman of the International Telephone and Telegraph Corporation (ITT), a company he helped build to revenues of about $17 billion before retiring in 1979, said of sweat capital, "In the business world everyone is paid in two coins: cash and experience. Take the experience first; the cash will come later."[8]

Whichever form of capital or mix of capital is decided upon, capital will always be important to making money in any terrain, so the Junglepreneur must always keep abreast of all the intricacies of capital.

Learn to Sell Well

Finally, making money requires the ability to sell very well. All of your efforts and processes will result in selling a good product or service at some point, so the Junglepreneur cannot avoid the selling process and must learn all its intricacies. The selling process itself involves marketing, advertising, promotion, proposition, and sales. Harry Gordon Selfridge, founder of Selfridges, was reputed to be very good at selling. One of his favorite quotes was, "It's business as usual. Keep on advertising." The words *sell* or *selling* bring about different positive or negative emotions from different people. The Junglepreneur must always find ways to bring out the positive aspects of selling and ensure the customer always comes away with a good experience. Selfridge and his former employer and mentor, Marshal Field, the founder of Marshal Field and Company, were both credited with coining the phrase *The customer is always right*. This was in a bid to emphasize the importance of the buying customer to the sales process. Marshal Field himself was a great believer in the sales process, and through this he built his Chicago department stores into a very successful chain of stores all over America.[9] Marshal Field and Company was bought recently by Macy's, and the former Marshal Field headquarters building in Chicago is now one of Macy's four national flagship stores.[10]

To achieve a good sales experience for the customer, the Junglepreneur should only sell good products or services that the Junglepreneur knows well and can deliver excellent service in. This gives the confidence to address any negative emotions that potential customers or clients may feel when being sold to. The Junglepreneur must develop the personal skills to sell well and then find people who also possess these skills to join the team. In developing the personal ability to sell, it will be useful to go for sales training regularly, have a mentor who is an expert in sales, and build up confidence against rejection through routine and repetition. Selling is a numbers game, and probability plays a big part. So reaching a greater number of people with sales calls on a regular basis increases the chances of making more sales.

This chapter has been about money and how it can be made in any terrain, and we now move on to the last component of the Junglepreneur MINEKIT.

Chapter Eight Takeaway: Junglepreneur Money Pipes

- No matter how rough or tough the terrain is, there is money to be made all around, and it is closer than you think.
- Decide to get a piece of the pie by doing all it takes to make money legally. Make money by taking a closer look to see opportunities, and follow where and how money flows in your terrain.
- Identify income streams, big spending patterns, and the market dynamics in your terrain to see how you can connect to the income streams.
- Connect by constructing your Junglepreneur Money Pipes, which are systems that efficiently produce and deliver your products and services of good value at the least cost to a large number of customers regularly.
- Identify your skills, and with focus and courage, apply them to the construction and implementation of your Junglepreneur Money Pipes so you maximize your income-earning potential.
- Go for your own business big game in your career at least once. This is like a big vision or large business project that will generate large, consistent, and enduring cash flow and income for you.
- Have a bread-and-butter backup survival strategy that you can fall back on for short-cycle cash flows. Do this by having at least one cash-based business that brings income on a regular basis, like retail, food, or transportation.
- Avoid your business systems halting by making all legal efforts to keep cash constantly flowing in and out of your business in a cash-flow cycle.
- Ensure you raise different kinds of capital for your business—like cash, asset, or sweat—for balance. The greatest capital, however, is you: your reputation and the confidence others have in your abilities.
- Make money by mastering the selling process, involving product knowledge, pricing, marketing, delivery, and post-sales service.

Nine
Traits of the Junglepreneur

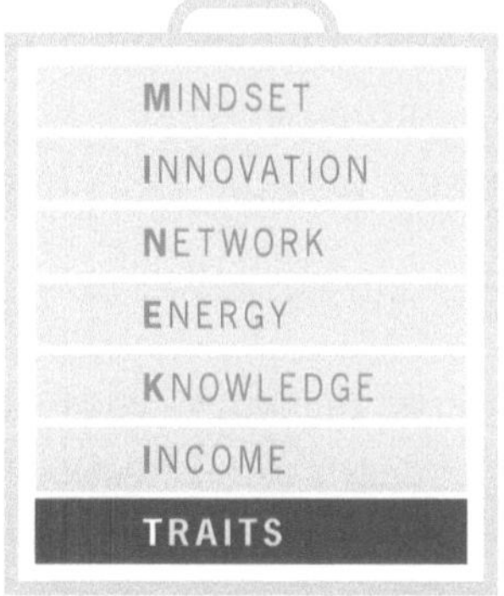

Every morning, an impala wakes up in the jungle, knowing that it must outrun the fastest lion that day if it wants to stay alive. Every morning a lion wakes up in the jungle knowing that it must outrun the slowest impala that day, or it will starve. It makes no difference if you are a lion or an impala; when the sun comes up in the jungle, you must wake up running.
—Adapted by the author from an African proverb

Your traits as a Junglepreneur are unique because, upon waking up every day, those traits have to be dependable enough to enable you to survive and thrive, and this is the important *T*, the final component of the Junglepreneur MINEKIT. I have also coined the Junglepreneurship traits as your Junglepreneur Person-Specific Assets, or Junglepreneur PSA. However, despite the appellation, they are not just an esoteric set of human characteristics. These traits really are very necessary to survive the tough business jungle, and they do have real meaning. You will need to acquire the Junglepreneur traits, as they have applicability to your success in the jungle. Acquiring these traits, or Junglepreneur PSA, enables you to derive maximum benefit through them for each and every passing moment of every single day. In many instances, these Junglepreneurship traits have a life-and-death meaning to the economic prosperity and even the physical survival of the Junglepreneur in tough terrains. Note that some readers may already possess some traits that have been proved useful, but even in such cases, those traits still need to be honed constantly to achieve more in the terrain. So what are these Junglepreneur traits, and how can they be acquired? Let us find out.

Utilize Willpower

Willpower is the ability to maximize your decision-making ability by utilizing your inner strength to take action in a desired direction. Willpower is necessary to overcome obstacles and achieve discipline, goals, and objectives. Willpower is what is required to be ready to go the extra mile to get to the resources necessary for survival.

Willpower is critical to survival in the business jungle, where the situation may make extreme demands on one's ability to persevere. For instance, in hot deserts you lose moisture and sweat so fast you don't even know it. It is the same in tough business environments, as the terrain can drain your very life essence. So, therefore, the Junglepreneur must have the strength and willpower to continue. In this regard, the Junglepreneur can be likened to a warrior or soldier trained in the disciplined survival tactics of such perilous situations as the jungle might bring. Therefore, the Junglepreneur has the survival mindset and willpower of a disciplined warrior.

Going Against Giants: Alpesh Patel offers an example of what willpower can achieve. Alpesh was the African sales director of one of the largest mobile-phone manufacturers in the world. Then against all odds he resigned in 2007 to set up his own mobile-phone manufacturing company. His vision was to sell his own brand of good-quality, low-cost mobile phones to the mass market in Africa. Operating out of Mauritius and manufacturing in China, Alpesh was thus on a collision course to compete against the large, entrenched, and better-funded phone manufacturers in the market.[1] For such an uphill task, he had to reach within himself to find the willpower to take the necessary action to make his vision come true. These actions included funding the business from his own savings, motivating a very hardworking team, doing innovative grassroots marketing, and running an almost 24-hour operation. Alpesh also decided to focus on making the phone a purely African brand and eventually called it Mi-Fone. In the course of the next five years, he went to great lengths to market the phone all over the continent. Mi-Fone has now sold close to two million handsets with great brand identification, as it is seen as the luxurious phone for the African mass market. Alpesh Patel could not have taken all the steps he took and achieved this level of success if he did not possess enough willpower to see through all the obstacles, no matter the odds.

Activate Discipline

To explain discipline, let me use this instance. Assuming you came across a harmful drink that you were informed was potentially fatal, would you drink it? Chances are that most likely you would not drink it; you would find it in yourself to reject that drink. So you already possess at least a minimum level of discipline, which has its foundations in willpower. Nevertheless, discipline sometimes needs to be consciously activated to motivate appropriate behavior in the face of basic human desires, instincts, or emotions, which may not be in line with your vision, beliefs, or purpose. However, a low level of discipline cannot be accommodated for a Junglepreneur, as discipline is a critical component of the law of survival. Discipline is required in the business jungle just as it is the natural jungle, as even wild animals can exhibit high discipline, as seen in primates.

Monkeys particularly have been observed to possess strict discipline, despite their playful nature. In the wild, a hierarchical leadership system is maintained by the head monkey. The head monkey is personally disciplined, oftentimes stern and cold. To get the clan in line, the head monkey will not hesitate to smack any misbehaving male, female, or baby. He does this so that when food becomes available, all the monkeys in the group will be disciplined enough not to be gluttonous and will allow others to feed. Obviously, humans are of a much higher nature than monkeys, and therefore it is possible and necessary for the Junglepreneur to operate at the highest levels of discipline required. Achieving high levels of discipline involves first determining the high standards that you aspire to for different scenarios. Then decide to hold yourself accountable to these standards. Better still, find another person you respect, a peer group or an institution that can hold you accountable to those standards you have set.

Deploy Adaptability

In conquering tough terrains, the Junglepreneur cannot afford to waste precious time wishing for the ideal circumstances to be made available. Due to the unpredictable nature of the business jungle, rarely will there be completely perfect situations. So the Junglepreneur must be flexible and adaptable to the stark realities on the ground. Adaptability is being nimble and savvy enough to maximize every little opportunity as leverage to gain higher resources or advantage. Adaptability means being pragmatic and practical enough to use what resources are presently available to meet the immediate needs and then build up from there to achieve the overall purpose. A good analogy for adaptability is cormorant fishing.

Cormorant fishing is a practice developed by fishermen in Japan and China, who have adapted to deep-water conditions by training cormorant birds to do their fishing for them. Cormorant birds are large, long-necked sea birds that weigh about 4 kilos (about 8.8 pounds), swim well, can naturally dive up to 30 meters under water, and can stay under water for well over a minute. They are experts at catching fish underwater for food. Asian fishermen long ago noticed these unique traits about the cormorant and thereby developed cormorant fishing. The technique of cormorant fishing, which is called *ukai* in Japanese, involves tying a string around the cormorant bird's neck so it can only swallow small fish for its own food. It is then released to the water to fish. When it catches large fish, it cannot swallow them. The fishermen pick these fish out of the bird's throat as their own catch. Through this process, the fishermen have adapted to their environment and used naturally occurring birds to catch the fish they sell to earn a living.[2]

Profitable Adaptation: A company in Brazil has built a huge business out of adapting to its environment by using bugs to aid farmers. Brazil is one of the most flexible places in the world to do business, but it faces major threats to its multi-billion dollar sugarcane and soybean plantations due to pests like the stinkbug and sugarcane borer. Traditionally, pesticides were used to fight the pests, but the effects of the pesticides are damaging to the environment. The Brazilian authorities decided to phase them out gradually. So Bugs Agentes Biologicos, a biotechnology company in Brazil, devised a way to adapt to changing regulatory policies by using what was already in the natural environment to solve the problem. They found out that the pests have a natural predator in the local wasps, so Bugs Agentes found a way to mass-breed the wasps to counter the pests and eliminate the use of pesticides altogether.[3]

Display Competent Behavior

In the business jungle, the behavior of the Junglepreneur is vital in how you relate to other people, attract them, and keep them close. Behavior is also about how you carry or conduct yourself through speech and action, the level of respect you give to yourself and others, how much interest you show in other people, and how much you care about their issues. We all have different behavioral patterns. However, no matter our individual idiosyncrasies, the goal is to try to attract and retain people as vital allies.

Though the Junglepreneur is meant to be tough, the basics required in attracting and retaining people as good friends and contacts include being friendly, supportive, and dependable. Note that in achieving this you do not necessarily have to fall over backwards to please people, as you still need to maintain some measure of self-respect. However, the Junglepreneur does need to be approachable and make people comfortable enough to seek out the presence of the Junglepreneur. The great poet Walt Whitman said that we convince by our presence, so it is all about well-placed confidence and making people feel safe and secure with you. It is not just about making people feel safe and believe that you can deliver; it is more about actually being able to deliver no matter what. For example, the late Steve Jobs of Apple was someone whose ability to deliver high value made his stakeholders believe very much in him.[4] When Jobs launched a new product, the launch presentation was always overbooked and covered as a media event. Apple customers all over the world would queue for hours waiting to buy the new product, partly due to their faith in Jobs's vision.[5]

The Junglepreneur works hard to build up well-deserved confidence and earns trust as the person needed to make things happen. If the Junglepreneur can achieve this, then access will be gained to great places and great people one could only have imagined. People who trust you will go the extra mile to help you, even using their own skills, talents, and personal network. They will share vital information, knowledge, and opportunities with you, all of which will determine your level of success in the business jungle. When I was managing the IT security firm in Nigeria, I recall the time we wanted to introduce some biometric solutions to a leading financial institution. Biometric products were relatively new to this market then, but using personal contacts, we got the institution to invite us for a presentation and demonstration. At that time my firm consisted of just four people as full-time staff, and we were meant to meet with the joint technology and management team of this large organization. I was scared that maybe we had gone way beyond our league and would fall flat on our faces. Then I remembered a friend of mine who was a technology guru and had too many certifications to count. There was also another much older friend who in his own right was the Chief Operating Officer of another large financial institution. They both did not have any stake in my organization, and against all odds, I convinced them to accompany my team to the presentation as part of our business team. They agreed simply because our friendship seemed to have some value in their eyes. When we got to the presentation, the institution had assembled their best team, as they wanted to take a nationwide decision concerning the biometric products. I gave my presentation and expected to be annihilated during question time. As expected they bombarded me with questions, but guess what? I hardly needed to speak, as my two friends went to bat for me and fended off all the technical and managerial questions until everyone in the room—including me—was in awe. The financial institution approved our proposal, and we successfully deployed in their major locations. The referrals from that contract got us seven-figure jobs in other places, and this momentum also opened up opportunities in other business areas. I am so grateful for having such people around me at such times.

Hone Instincts and Be Alert

Instinct is a personal internal warning system, which needs to be developed and honed. The Junglepreneur must be very aware of his or her own instincts and become very sensitive to them. Instinct is the sixth sense, which resides in the subconscious mind and which nature has given to us to warn of danger that may not be perceived by our other sensory organs. Instinct should be taken very seriously in business, as it will guide well and provide ideas, solutions, and insight that one may not have had otherwise.

It is likely that the instincts of the businessman in our diamonds story warned him about the diamond transaction, but maybe he was not sensitive enough to notice or maybe he even ignored his instincts completely, probably due to greed. If one senses that a business situation does not feel right, then it probably is not. If a transaction feels dodgy, it probably is, so check again. In the business jungle, the law is *look before you leap*, so you can be sure of not jumping over a cliff. Most times your instincts will give off warnings to look closely at where you want to jump. Cultivate your instinct by taking time to observe closely for hidden cues that your immediate environment will give off. In developing instinct, it is also useful to train yourself to be still, quiet, and just listen to your inner self.

Instinct and alertness go hand in hand. B.C. Forbes, the late owner of *Forbes* magazine, said that "judgment can be acquired only by acute observation, by actual experience in the school of life, by ceaseless alertness to learn from others."[6] The environment is at all times giving out information, energy, resources, and stimuli, which are necessary for the creative process. The Junglepreneur needs to be mentally alert at all times by using all the senses to perceive, receive, and process all that the environment is giving off. Curiosity is a key component of mental alertness, as the act of being curious helps to start the process itself. In exhibiting curiosity it is important that you are careful not to be intrusive on the rights or privacy of others or break any laws. Rather, curiosity is more concerned with taking note of the unusual and investigating further anything that strikes you as being different from normality. Nobel laureate Albert Einstein said concerning curiosity, "The important thing is not to stop questioning ... curiosity has its own reason for existing... One cannot help but be in awe when he contemplates the mysteries of eternity, of life, of the marvelous structure of reality."[7]

Attain High Physical Stamina

The business jungle requires physical efforts in achieving goals, and this requires a great deal of physical fitness. There will be the need to travel around on various trips, go for numerous meetings, and work long hours, so the Junglepreneur has to take every step to be physically fit and healthy at all cost. This is very important to success, as ill health or lethargy can cost more than one realizes, since valuable time can be lost.

Being unfit also means one may tire faster and one's work will suffer. Since the body is not used to this system of strain, symptoms of stress may develop along with its health complications. Business itself is already a highly charged atmosphere, and a physical channel like exercise is required to work out negative emotions like exasperation that may have accumulated. Exercise can also be therapeutic; for instance, you can visualize a tough obstacle facing you as a punching bag and go to the gym to have a boxing session. While imagining the punching bag as the obstacle, you'll be amazed how powerless it becomes to your mind. Or better still, imagine the obstacle as a golf ball, tennis ball, football, or any other sporting ball you fancy. Go to the driving range, tennis court, or playing field and hit some balls. Picture the balls as that stubborn problem or challenge you are facing, and let out some steam from your system by hitting those balls really hard. You may find out that this may actually calm any frayed nerves you have. The physical activity for you may even be a useful process for opening up your mind to other possible solutions while you are engrossed in your exercise.

Ingrain Perseverance

It is said the road to success has many parking lots along the way, and there is the temptation to just park and forget it all. Perseverance or persistence can become a golden advantage that enables the Junglepreneur to outlast any situation if deployed well.

> The US Navy SEALS—an elite sea, air, and land special fighting force of the US Navy—have a creed, which is their code of conduct and statement of commitment to affirm their decisions to be SEALS. This unique warrior creed reads in part: "Forged by adversity … I will never quit. I persevere and thrive on adversity … If knocked down, I will get back up, every time … I am never out of the fight."[8]

The important thing to know about persistence or perseverance is that it is not just a skill learned or knowledge acquired. Rather, perseverance also comes from taking a firm and irrevocable decision to continue on the path you have chosen, regardless of any challenge or obstacle you may face. Through perseverance the Junglepreneur becomes an innovative and risk-embracing person who, even in extremely challenging situations, will somehow survive and thrive.

A major point of note here, however, is for the Junglepreneur to be absolutely sure that the right path has been chosen in the first place. Social reformer and public speaker Henry Ward Beecher identified the difference between perseverance and obstinacy by observing that perseverance evolves from a strong will, while obstinacy comes from a strong won't.[9] So apply your will by deciding to keep persevering and slugging on, no matter how tough it may seem, but be sure the path is worth the struggle. It has been noted by nature explorers who have traveled in heavy snow conditions that one of the best things to do when exposed to a snow blizzard or storm is to keep moving. Otherwise, one gets covered over by the snow storm.

Perseverance means facing down some resistance from our mind, from the environment, or from others. To overcome this resistance and keep persevering, you must continuously commit to making your effort for just one more time. You can keep up the continuity of trying by rewarding yourself in a small way for each time you keep trying. This way, your efforts will become like a constant drip of acid, which will eventually wear away at any obstacle.

The Ford Perseverance: Henry Ford, the founder of the Ford Motor Company, was a man who persevered in the face of daunting challenges.[10] In the early days of the company, around 1930, Ford told his engineers that he wanted to build the first single-cast V8 engine, which would be used for a low-priced and affordable car. His engineers told him this type of engine had never built before in a single cast and was impossible. Rather than being discouraged, Ford simply told them to go ahead and do it. Even after they came back repeatedly to tell him it could not be done, Ford simply told them produce it anyway. Eventually his engineers found a way to give Henry Ford the single-cast V8 engine he desired for the masses, and thereby he made an affordable V8 car. The Ford Motor Company benefitted immensely from this success and went on to become a leading automobile company in the world, which it still is today.

The Wright brothers, Orville and Wilbur, even after several failures, still persevered until they built the world's first powered and controlled plane on December 17, 1903, in Kitty Hawk, North Carolina.[11] The American inventor Thomas Edison is arguably the greatest inventor of all time due to the large number of patents he registered and inventions he pioneered.[12] However, even he had to continually persevere, after many failures, until he gave the world the first light bulb in 1879 and helped to lay the foundations of the electrical industry.

Perseverance or persistence is that fire that burns away every form of impurity from your goal. You can never lose from persevering. After your persistence has won the day, it reveals in you a fine character that will serve you well in the future. Persevering may be hard but as long as you are sure you are in the right direction, keep on moving, be in constant motion, and keep on keeping on.

Exhibit Self-Control

Self-control, on the other hand, is the ability to exercise mastery over your desires, needs, and wants, no matter how important they may present themselves as being. It is also the ability to forgo or delay personal gratification. In the business jungle, this ability will serve you well, as you'll know how to control yourself and resist the urge to take an action that may eventually prove fatal. Experienced seamen say that when shipwrecked, the ability to resist drinking the seawater will determine one's survival, because seawater is extremely salty and will dehydrate the body to a swift death.

Self-control itself stems from the ability to maintain calmness. Calmness is being able to remain unhurried, keep a level head, and think straight when in a tight spot. It is the sailor's ability to remain calm in the face of a raging storm that guarantees the survival of the whole ship and crew. Sailors also know that the raging sea storm is usually only on the surface, as most storms rarely go beyond 400 meters below the surface of the sea. After that point, all is actually well beneath the sea, so at that instance, if they have heavy and extra anchors, the sailors may decide to drop anchor and wait out the storm, as they may stand a greater chance of survival if the anchored boat responds better to changes in the wind and water.

The Junglepreneur must develop the capacity to remain calm and unhurried without being dull or lazy. Note that you can move swiftly without being hurried, as moving swiftly is also essential to success. Being calm and unhurried does not mean being slow or failing to take action in the right time. Being calm and unhurried means moving at the right pace and speed required to maximize all opportunities needed for optimum success at that point in time.

Traits, *T*, concludes the Junglepreneur MINEKIT, which started with mindset and moved through innovation, network, energy, knowledge, and income. Now you are empowered to tackle and tame any tough business terrain in any location. However, there is one more thing you need to complement the kit, and that's attitude. This is because even if you have the best tools, they still need to be used with the right attitude, or else they will be ineffective. The attitudes you require to use the Junglepreneur MINEKIT successfully will ensure that you can tame any tough terrain. This is all in the next and final chapter.

Chapter Nine Takeaway: Winning Traits

- Acquire or hone your Junglepreneur traits, or Junglepreneur Person-Specific Assets (PSA), to derive maximum benefit through them for each and every passing moment of every single day in the business jungle.
- Utilize willpower to overcome obstacles, maximize decision making, and achieve set goals in your tough terrain.
- Activate discipline consciously to stimulate the behavior necessary for achieving your business purpose, despite basic human desires and emotions.
- Exercise adaptability in your tough terrain by being flexible, pragmatic, and nimble enough to leverage every little opportunity to gain higher value.
- Display competent behavior to attract people and relate well with vital allies in your terrain. Do this by caring and conducting yourself well in speech and action.
- Hone your instinct so it serves you well as an internal warning system in your terrain. Do this by being sensitive to internal alarm bells in business situations. If it does not feel right, then it probably is not.
- Gain high stamina needed to cope with physical and mental demands of tough terrain. Exercise regularly to gain this stamina and thus avoid lethargy or ill health, which could limit your abilities for success.
- Establish perseverance in your efforts by deciding to resist limitations from your environment. Commit to making one more effort continuously toward your vision, and reward yourself for this.
- Exercise self-control over desires, needs, and wants that are not in line with your vision. Delay personal gratification, and maintain calmness and a level head when things get out of control.

Ten
The Junglepreneur's Attitude

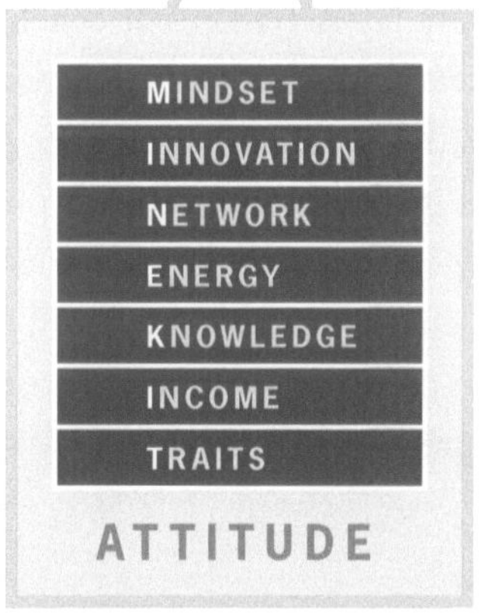

Success or failure in business is caused more by the mental attitude even than by mental capacities.
—Sir Walter Scott

The greatest discovery of all time is that a person can change his future by merely changing his attitude.
—Oprah Winfrey

At any given time, attitudes can influence your behavior consciously or unconsciously, and they can also influence the way you will use the Junglepreneur MINEKIT. Attitudes are influenced by our ideas, beliefs, and values and developed through our learning, experiences, and emotions. Even more than ability, attitude is the key determinant of success, and it will also determine how effectively you use the kit and the level of results you will get. Charles Swindol, an author and Christian preacher, describes attitude as being more important than skills, gifts, your past, what people say, education, what people do, money, looks, gifts, or skills. For the Junglepreneur, it is important to cultivate a positive attitude.

When the Junglepreneur is faced with negative attitudes either personally or in others, it is important to know that change is possible. Find a way to influence the underlying emotions that control the said attitude, and at the end of the day, you may achieve a positive and great attitude. The great NBA basketball coach Pat Riley, who once coached both LA Lakers and New York Knicks, described a positive attitude as giving one the ability to overcome present problems and face greater challenges in the future.[1] Riley's positive attitude helped him to overcome many coaching challenges, and he is named as one of the ten best basketball coaches of all time. I will now consider in detail more elements of what constitutes the great attitude that you need to implement the Junglepreneur MINEKIT.

Show Courage

Courage is said to be the ability to overcome fear and still take action. Giving attention to fear will distract the Junglepreneur from the vision of becoming successful. Samuel Langhorne Clemens is the author also known as Mark Twain, who wrote popular books like *The Adventures of Tom Sawyer* and *The Adventures of Huckleberry Finn*.[2] Mark Twain described courage as not the absence of fear but the resisting and mastering of fear. The Junglepreneur will feel great fear at some point on the journey in the business jungle, but it must be overcome. There will be times when the Junglepreneur will encounter huge challenges and seem lost, without help and with just no way out. It is at these times that your instinct filters your choice down to two options often dictated by nature. Either you will battle it out against the problems or scuttle away from them in fear.

The Junglepreneur has to decide which option to choose and determine not to make the choice based on fear. Instead, he should choose based on the need for survival.

In the jungle when an animal exhibits fear, it often releases a chemical or hormone, which has a distinctive smell that certain animals or insects can sense. Those animals that sense it attack the fearful animal. A bee stings mainly when it perceives a fear odor emanating from its victim. Before fighting over territory or mating partners, male monkeys will sniff out each other first to detect fear. If one monkey perceives weakness in the other monkey, it will attack the other immediately.

The principle of fear works in a similar way in the business jungle. Once a person exhibits fear, the signal goes out, and it unconsciously shows in the actions, reactions, speech, posture, and mannerisms. Others will often pick it up immediately and react. The Junglepreneur's ability to handle fear can determine success or failure, so the Junglepreneur must perk up, be courageous, and show confidence even if he or she doesn't feel like it. During the times when you really do not have any courage, at least attempt to act it, and after some time the mind will not know the difference.

The bobcat is a small predatory cat that lives in the wild and is very good at showing confidence when in great danger. Though bobcats only weigh between 12 and 23kg (26 to 50 pounds), depending on the species, they have been known to charge and chase away lions or jaguars many times bigger than themselves when attacked by the larger animals.

To build up more courage, the Junglepreneur will do well to also get some profiles of courage and gain inspiration. A sterling example of a profile of courage and dignity is the life of the late Nelson Mandela, who survived very challenging situations, as will be discussed in the next section.

Maintain Dignity

The Junglepreneur must always maintain dignity and also treat others with dignity. Dignity is self-respect and an internal benchmark of poise and calmness. Dignity is the unique ability to remain stoic in the face of challenges by repressing any unnecessary display of negative emotion. Dignity is the grace and strength to exhibit patient endurance in the face of adversity and yet remain inspiring rather than cold or distant.

Even in the toughest of times and messiest of situations, the Junglepreneur must maintain dignity always and by all means. Even if it does not serve any other purpose, maintaining dignity will at least deprive your adversaries of the joy of seeing you grovel or demean yourself. However, it does serve a greater purpose, as maintaining dignity sets the Junglepreneur apart as a noble soul worthy of respect. Even if they don't admit it, those around you—even your adversaries—will really take notice.

Nelson Rolihlahla Mandela (1918–2013) of South Africa was a freedom fighter of the African National Congress (ANC) who fought against the apartheid regime of South Africa. For this, Mandela was jailed in 1962 for sabotage, and he served in prison for 27 years, mostly with hard labor.[3] In prison on Robben Island, Mandela's favorite poem, which he often read to himself and other prisoners, was the "Invictus":

Out of the night that covers me,
Black as the Pit from pole to pole,
I thank whatever Gods may be
For my unconquerable soul.

In the fell clutch of circumstance,
I have not winced nor cried aloud,
Under the bludgeoning of chance

My head is bloody but unbowed.
Beyond this place of wrath and tears
Looms but the horror of the shade,
And yet the menace of the years
Finds, and shall find, me unafraid.

It matters not how strait the gate,
How charged with punishments the scroll.
I am the master of my fate:
I am the captain of my soul.

While in prison he was made to do all sorts of degrading, menial work, but through it all, he maintained his dignity and eventually won the respect of his captors. When the time came for him to be released from prison on his own terms in 1990, Mandela had negotiated the end of apartheid in South Africa. In 1994, South Africa voted in a democratic election and considered Nelson Mandela worthy and noble enough to be their elected president under a new constitution. While president, he remained noble and gracious enough to forgive all his adversaries. He shunned revenge and healed the entire nation of deep wounds, resulting in a new national bonding, synergy, and greatness for South Africa. A visit to the apartheid museum in South Africa is a lesson in history, and one will come away with an immense appreciation of the level of great sacrifice, forgiveness, and dignity displayed by Mandela.[4] Nelson Mandela remains the father of the South African nation and was a recipient of the Nobel Peace Prize. Upon his death in 2013, leaders from all over the world gathered in South Africa to mourn his passing in a grand and moving ceremony.

The poem "Invictus" (Latin for *unconquered*), which inspired Nelson Mandela, was written by an Englishman named William Ernest Henley (1849–1903).[5] Henley himself had faced great adversity in life and had relied on stoicism to see him through. Henley contracted tuberculosis in his teenage years and had to have one of his legs amputated. The second was under threat of amputation too but was eventually saved. It was a tough time in Henley's life, during which he reflected on his impoverished childhood and was moved to write "Invictus." Like Henley and Mandela, the Junglepreneur must maintain dignity no matter the circumstances. Remember that if you must go down at all, go down with your head held high. However, even if the Junglepreneur goes down, he will most certainly rise again because of the Junglepreneur's innate qualities of success.

Display Confidence

Sometimes the major obstacle we face on our way to success is lack of confidence and belief in ourselves. It may come from negative self-narratives, doubt, or long-held convictions about the limitations that exist regarding our goals. These are commonly called limiting beliefs. Norman Vincent Peale, author of the popular book *The Power of Positive Thinking*, says, "Believe in yourself! Have faith in your abilities! Without a humble confidence in your own powers, you cannot be successful or happy."[6] In trying to do what Peale says, the Junglepreneur should be particularly sensitive to negative self-narratives, which may include thoughts about not being good enough, why one cannot achieve what is desired, or how one may be lacking in abilities. The Junglepreneur should be watchful when faced with myriad problems, as thoughts tend to gravitate toward the problems alone, giving them all the attention rather than working on solutions or new progressive goals. All these can lead to a state of low confidence in one's personal ability to achieve. However, no matter the limitations faced by the Junglepreneur, confidence will surmount them.

Helen Keller (1880–1968) became deaf and blind at two years old after contracting a childhood illness. Yet with the help of her teacher, Anne Sullivan, Helen learned to communicate by understanding speech through the touch of her hands. In this way, Helen Keller became the first deaf and blind person to earn a Bachelor of Arts degree from a university and went on to become a world-famous author and speaker. Helen Keller, who became a true inspiration for many, attributed optimism, hope, and confidence to be the beliefs and characteristics that ensure achievement.[7]

What the mind tells us is based on what it has been exposed to and what it has been told all through our lives. This information determines confidence levels. So if the mind has been pre-programmed with wrong or bad information, it will default toward negative self-narratives and low self-confidence. The Junglepreneur must change any negatives to positives through self-affirmation to achieve high self-confidence.

Have Expectations

Every human has an internal level of expectation regarding success and what they can achieve. This internal level of expectation has been set by the program the mind is running based on narratives. This may often not be based on the actual potential—which may be immense—but it is often based on what people have told themselves or what others may have told them about their abilities or inabilities. This results in each person having an internal ability thermostat set by narratives. A real thermostat will regulate the temperature of a building by increasing or decreasing the temperature. In the same way, your internal ability thermostat will regulate the success you are able to achieve, through narratives in the subconscious mind. If wrongly set to a low level, the ability thermostat will actively reduce achievements, using the subconscious mind. It does this through self-sabotaging behavior like procrastination, negative self-talk, avoidance, discouragement, delay, lack of commitment, indiscipline, etc. These are simply ways in which the subconscious mind is trying to protect you from what it perceives as too much success for your internal ability to handle.

The Junglepreneur needs to find out if his internal ability thermostat has been set at the right level, based on his actual potential and abilities. If the internal ability thermostat is set too low or too high, it needs to be reset based on realistic potential. The Junglepreneur's true potential can be discovered after carrying out an audit of personal abilities, opportunities, and weaknesses, as seen in an earlier chapter. Note after the self-audit that you do not focus on your weaknesses, but rather you should conduct a personal-development program, which will focus mainly on strengthening abilities. The internal ability thermostat can also be reset through personal-development techniques such as setting new goals, positive self-talk, affirmations, and visualization.

Get Motivation

To succeed, the Junglepreneur needs a constant stream of large amounts of energy and drive that is produced internally. This constant stream of energy is what is used to take massive and consistent action toward achieving great goals. Self-motivation is what fuels this stream of energy, like an engine system that generates constant energy to keep going. Self-motivation is like an internal force that drives and pushes the Junglepreneur upwards toward goals and objectives.

Reaching $1 Billion Through Motivation: In 1914, Thomas J. Watson was hired by the Computing Tabulating Recording company (CTR) as a general manager. Fewer than five years later, he had doubled the company revenues from US$5 million to about US$10 million. By 1925, Watson had rebuilt CTR into what became known as International Business Machines, or IBM.[8] By the time Thomas Watson died in 1956, he had led IBM as its president and chairman to be a company with almost $1 billion revenue and about 70,000 employees. IBM is still a global technology force today, and the company has recently launched an artificial-intelligence program bearing Watson's name. Watson, who was considered the best salesman in the world in his time, offered this bit of advice before his passing: "Nothing so conclusively proves a man's ability to lead others as what he does day-to-day to lead himself."

Finding self-motivation is easier said than done. Humans naturally like to revert to their most comfortable state, which is often lethargy. It can be very easy to get discouraged in the face of obstacles or challenges. So how does one build self-motivation? To get self-motivation, the Junglepreneur can use some of the following techniques.

Emotional Anchors

Our emotional anchors are those things that we cherish and that mean the world to us. It may be a cause or belief that you hold so dearly or a loved one whom you value more than even yourself. A great amount of wealth and achievement in this world has come through people finding an emotional anchor to reach for a goal. So in seeking self-motivation, you should find an internal emotional anchor and begin to imagine the object of your affection in a better state as a result of you taking action toward your goals.

These images help release certain hormones and emotions in you, which are extremely powerful in moving your system to take action. So decide what your emotional anchor is and tie the achievement of your goal toward its betterment. This is what will give you that extra kick to take the next step when tired or to abstain from destructive habits. The emotional anchor is what pushes the Junglepreneur to work at odd hours or get up at 4 AM to work or practice when he or she could be enjoying sleep. It pushes the Junglepreneur to also sacrifice many pleasures or leisure activities just to carry out tasks necessary for moving forward in a vision.

Pain is Fuel

Hurt can be a useful fuel to produce energy to move the Junglepreneur forward. Sometimes when faced with challenges in business or other areas of our lives, we may be slighted, experience hurt, face pain, or even be embarrassed by people or institutions. It is not a time to take offense or get into fights but to use that pain as a perfect fuel for self-motivation to turn the negative into a positive. The Junglepreneur does this by finding out the goals, objectives, or achievements that have not been attained yet in the area where the slight or hurt occurred. Then the Junglepreneur should push forward into achieving those goals or objectives.

Anytime you feel like giving up, remember the pain of the experience, and find that extra strength to continue. However, using personal pain to fuel self-motivation should not result in carrying out vengeance on the offending party. Instead, it is fuel to help the Junglepreneur to succeed in the area found wanting. After all, resounding success is the sweetest form of self-fulfillment.

Success is Fuel

On the flip side, the Junglepreneur probably has had a lot of successes that can bring strong positive feelings when reminisced upon. These achievements are assets for stimulating those good, positive feelings about how fulfilling success can be. So when the Junglepreneur feels low or unmotivated, remember the sweet taste of success and keep pushing forward so you can achieve even more.

Gratitude

The late American social reformer and public speaker Henry Ward Beecher said, "Gratitude is the fairest blossom which springs from the soul."[9] You should cultivate the habit of taking a good look around to count your own blessings. For certain there will be some good things in your life that you can be thankful to God or your higher belief for. It could be good health, family, friends, education, opportunities, resources, skills, etc. Identify these blessings, and have a grateful heart to Omnipotent power and the universe for giving them to you sometimes even undeservedly. Though you may have present challenges, the fact that you have these blessings is a sure sign that more will come in the future.

See the Bright Side

It is said that there are two sets of people in life: those who see a glass of water as being half empty and those who see it as being half full. There are also those who will look at a doughnut and see only a delicious treat to be relished, while others will look and only see the hole in the middle. This is simply a way of describing the contrast between pessimism and optimism.

Half of the water in the glass may be gone in reality, but instead of complaining over the half that is gone, recognize that the glass is still half full. Eagerly anticipate the enjoyment of the other half still left in the glass. Likewise, a doughnut may have a hole at the center, but it still is yummy. Go on and enjoy it! On the flip side of a dark and miserable cloud is bright sunshine, which will soon break forth. So despite whatever issues you are facing, you should always try to see the brighter side of things and enjoy what life has to offer presently.

Take Action

Once you are well-motivated, physical action is then required to be taken before goals can be achieved. This is an area of great struggle for many, but it is where the Junglepreneur must excel. Thomas Jefferson, one of the authors of the American Declaration of Independence and America's third president, is quoted as saying, "Do you want to know who you are? Don't ask. Act! Action will delineate and define you."[10] On the other hand, not taking action, by delaying unduly or averting it, is deemed to be procrastination. Time marches on like a soldier, but procrastination is like a spectator who watches the time marching on. It often stems from many reasons, such as:

- Indecision about the order of importance of tasks or which task to do first,
- Unwillingness to disturb present pleasure by doing the task now,
- Wrong belief that there is enough time to do the task later,
- Fear of the stress that doing the task will bring,
- Over analyzing or over simplifying the task,
- Not allocating a specific time slot and duration for doing the task,
- False acceptance that the task may not be necessary at all,
- Doubt about one's ability or knowledge to do the task,
- Waiting for the perfect circumstances to do the task,
- Incorrect conviction that the task may get easier with time if one waits,
- Preoccupation with too many other tasks,
- Possibility of delegating the task away eventually,
- Uncertainty about the task's necessity in achieving the goal, or
- Lack of available effort or concentration to accomplish the task now.

All these reasons or more may eventually lead to the task never getting done. To avoid procrastination, it would help to have a check-list for most of the tasks that need to be done each day, week, and month. Next, order the tasks based on the level of importance and note if you need any extra help with getting them done. Then start taking action from whichever level or whatever imperfect state you are in. You can perfect things, or get more resources, as you go along, but simply get going first and start doing those tasks. Pablo Picasso (1881–1973), the prolific Spanish-born sculptor and painter, who produced over 40,000 different works of art in his lifetime, said, "Action is the fundamental key to all success."[11] For such a very active artist, he probably knew what he was talking about.

Seek Relaxation

In concluding this book, it will be necessary for me to talk about the need for the Junglepreneur to relax when necessary. The business terrain does require focused discipline and actions, but the Junglepreneur is not a stern, unpleasant workaholic. After all, the jungle can also be a lively, bubbly place, full of life, sights, and sounds. The Junglepreneur must learn to relax, laugh, exercise, eat well, and have plenty of fun. Even animals relax and have fun, and so should human beings. There is a story about a pair of house rabbits in Swindon, England, that has particular resonance on this point. Let's call it "The Tale of Two Rabbits."

The two rabbits in this tale are siblings named Charlie and Tommy. Being house rabbits, Charlie and Tommy were allowed to live freely in the yard and around the house, even though they also had rabbit hutches to sleep in. Despite their familial relation and similar living situation, they exhibited very different personalities. Tommy was withdrawn and often paranoid, running away from everyone, including his owners, and mainly preferring to keep to his cage. Charlie, on the other hand, was the exact opposite of Tommy: full of life, very friendly, inquisitive, fun-loving, adventurous, and fearless. Charlie could always be seen running around the garden or in the family house and generally seemed to enjoy his life. Both Charlie and Tommy were very well cared for with good, hygienic shelter, regular food, rabbit vaccinations, and veterinary treatments. However, Tommy eventually died of seemingly natural causes in 2011, having lived for only five human years. This was below the average life span for house rabbits, which is about eight to 10 human years. Charlie, on the other hand, lived for three more years and only recently died of natural causes in September 2014, at the ripe old age of eight human years. This is of course after living a good, mature, fun-filled and happy rabbit life.

Could the secret to Charlie's longevity be his friendly attitude and fun-loving lifestyle? It is probably so, and if a rabbit can enjoy this life, then why not humans? Moreover, if enjoying life has longevity implications for rabbits, then relaxing and having some fun will definitely be beneficial to the Junglepreneur, even if only as a stress reducer. World championship athlete Sasha Cohen also says, "Follow your dreams, work hard, practice, and persevere. Make sure you eat a variety of foods, get plenty of exercise, and maintain a healthy lifestyle." So after working hard, the Junglepreneur should take time out to play hard and enjoy life on a regular basis. After all, this is what makes all your effort worth it.

On a final note, you will recall that in the Introduction, I described the journey of the Junglepreneur through challenging environments. Note that it really does not matter which part of that journey you are in presently, but it does matter that you approach your journey in the right way, using the frameworks, tools, and concepts of the Junglepreneur. Doing this ensures that you will eventually achieve sustainable success, regardless of how demanding your terrain is. You already have all the resources, opportunities, and energy in you or around you; you just need to tap into them. You can do it. All you have to do is go for it. Keep trying, persevere, and don't give up. Keep mining that terrain until it yields its bounty for you. Continue pushing on until you become the king of the business jungle. You can do this because you now know the way of the Junglepreneur.

Chapter Ten Takeaway: Attitude for Success

- Your attitude influences your overall behavior and will influence how you will use the Junglepreneur MINEKIT.
- Exhibit courage to overcome fear and take action. Achieve this by giving no attention to fear so it does not distract you from becoming successful.
- Keep your dignity, and treat others with dignity. Show poise, calmness, grace, and strength in the face of challenges. Do this by remaining stoic even if you don't feel like it.
- Have confidence in your own abilities. Shun negative narratives, focus on your strengths, and use your past successes as proof of what you can achieve.
- Set your internal expectations at the right level, based on your actual potential and abilities. Discover your true potential by carrying out an audit of your personal abilities, opportunities, and weaknesses.
- Take action, and don't procrastinate. Your actions will define who you will be.
- Motivate yourself to succeed by tying this to emotional anchors that link to what you care about. Use your pain and success as fuel to greater heights.
- Relax, laugh, and have fun while working at your goals. Always see the brighter side of things, and enjoy the whole process of succeeding.

Conclusion
You are Jungle CAPABLE

My friend and veteran graphics designer, Ken Calcut, recently shared with me a favourite quote from his dear departed father, Thomas W. Calcut, who was a much loved British quip and humor artist. In his time, when Thomas felt he shared a deep affinity with someone, he often said "I know you, we went to different schools together". Having modified this quip with Ken's permission, I now say, "I know you, we went to different jungles together". The reason I love this modified quote so much, is that I really do feel an affinity with you because just like I have, you have also experienced your own jungle. This affinity is further strengthened because over the course of this book, we have considered many concepts together, starting with who you are, the nature of your business jungle, and how you can manage its complexities. This book has tried to be a voice in your ear as you go on to survive and thrive in tough business terrains. Having reached this point, you are now the embodiment of this person—the self-respecting, motivated Junglepreneur—of great courage and capability. I daresay that right now you are immensely Jungle CAPABLE because you have just honed your abilities to be creative, adaptable, persistent, aware, brave, linked, and energized. At this very moment, you are able to operate in any tough business terrain and succeed. You will be able to always do this when required because you remain teachable and will continue to seek knowledge on what to do in difficult circumstances.

Always remember that you, the Junglepreneur, are a person of great vision who sees streams where others see deserts. Remember that when others fear the future and always keep looking back at the past, you, the Junglepreneur, learn from the past and with courage and vision always keep looking forward to the future. Now is the time of the Junglepreneurs, and the future of the new business world belongs to you. Remember that you can survive and succeed in any business terrain in any location because you have the mindset, innovativeness, network, energy, knowledge, income, and traits to do so. You are also a relaxed, fun-loving person, who plays hard after working hard.

So, dear Junglepreneur, the ability is within you to successfully face any business terrain and overcome any challenge by deploying your energy to maximize resources and opportunities available to you. You just need to have positive expectations and believe they will happen. Now that you have completed reading this book, the very next steps you take will be extremely important. What to do next is to immediately begin to implement the Junglepreneur frameworks and information within your terrain today. It is also important to network with other Junglepreneurs who can share advice and experiences that can encourage you in your own journey. Don't delay, waiting for a perfect time; this is your perfect time. To help with these, first you can go to www.junglepreneur.com to get a copy of *Way of the Junglepreneur Workbook*, which is a supporting resource to this book. It contains detailed and practical exercises that you can carry out based on the knowledge you have acquired here. Furthermore, you can also visit the Junglepreneur website to network with other Junglepreneurs and to also access additional resources. I leave you with these words: Don't wait for things to happen. Always make them happen every day. Take all necessary action in the time that you have right now. I wish you every success, as I believe you can achieve it, and may the terrain favor you.

EPILOGUE

The Junglepreneur philosophy is transforming into a movement of people with like minds and is taking root in tough terrains all around the world. Junglepreneurs aim to conquer business jungles wherever they may exist, using the ever-evolving philosophy of the Junglepreneur.

We come together to encourage one another and share experiences, information, or ideas. Junglepreneurs are on the path to somewhere exciting, and if you feel a stir in your spirit, then you are most welcome to join us at www.Junglepreneur.com.

Bibliography and Notes

Chapter One

1 Fasanya, Oludotun. *The US Sub-Prime Mortgage Lending Crises, Subsequent Credit Crunch and their Effects on the UK Financial Systems: Where now for Financial Risk Management and Corporate Governance?*—A Case Study. Leicester Business School, UK. 2008.

2 Subprime Bank Losses Top $323 Billion. *Bloomberg News*. May 9, 2008. Http://www.bloomberg.com

3 Mellor, Mary. *The Future of Money: From Financial Crises to Public Resource*. London, Pluto, 2010.

4 Elon Musk's Hyperloop: San Francisco to Los Angeles in 30 Minutes? *Wall Street Journal*. August 12, 2013. http://online.wsj.com

5 Cash is for Losers, The Future of Mobile Payments is in Play. *Bloomberg-BusinessWeek*. November 24, 2014. Pp50.

6 Bitcoin Poised to Shake Up Government Run Currencies. *Financial Times*. October 5, 2014. http://www.ft.com/indepth/bitcoin

7 Armagnac, Alden. How Diamonds Rocketed from the Earth's Depths. *Popular Science*. 1973.Pp 60.

8 Yenne, Bill. The Story of the Boeing Company. (Revised and Updated Version). Zenith Press. USA. 2005.

9 New Boeing Jet, 777X, Hits $95 Billion in Orders. *New York Times*. November 17, 2013. http://www.nytimes.com

10 Mary Kay Ash. *The Mary Kay Way- Timeless Principles from America's Greatest Woman Entrepreneur*. 2009. John Wiley.

11 Eiji Toyoda. *Toyota 50 Years in Motion: An Autobiography*. Kodansha International. 1987.

12 Toyota Retains Number One Slot in Global Car Sales. *BBC News*. January 23, 2014. http://www.bbc.co.uk

13 Http://ethiopianflowerexport.com

Chapter Two

1 John Schermerhorn. *Introduction to Management.* John Wiley. 2011. Pp 336.

2 Street traders and traffic hold-ups similarly called 'Go-slow' also exist in Jamaica and parts of South America.

3 AngloGold Faces Enormous Challenges in Ghana. *Bloomberg News*. Jan 23, 2014. Http://www.bloomberg.com

4 The classification of tough business terrains is not exhaustive. There are categories that may not be included here but which are specific to certain terrains.

5 World Bank Ease of Doing Business Index: The index ranks global economies on a scale of 1 to 189. A score of 1 is the highest and means the regulatory environment is conducive for business operations. A score of 189 is the lowest and conversely indicates that the regulatory environment is not very conducive for business operations.

6 Bantu Investment following up Investments of R2bn in Congo. *Business Day Newspapers*, South Africa, August 6, 2012.

7 Marcus Aurelius Antoninus. *Meditations*. Rome. AD 121–180. Meditations is based on the lifestyle of Roman Emperor Marcus Aurelius and the philosophy of stoicism which argues for the attainment of personal discipline and the avoidance of vain or excessive pleasures.

8 This is based on discussions between the author and the manufacturer.

Chapter Three

1 Maslow, Abraham. *The Psychology of Science: A Reconnaissance.* Maurice Bassett Publishing. 1966.

2 Aside from knowledge tools, there are various categories of specialised

business tools and these include process tools, leadership tools, technology tools, strategy tools and financials tools among others. The knowledge tools discussed in Junglepreneur MINEKIT also cut across some of the others.

3 Mayer, Florian. *A Case Study of Easyjet and the Airline Industry*. GRIN, Verlag, Germany. 2003.

4 Britannica Book of the Year. *Encyclopedia Britannica.* 2014. Pp 356.

5 The author has observed this cash counting phenomenon in various street markets in Africa and even in the Middle-East. The system enables a trader to keep track of the banknotes being counted even during a conversation with a customer. This technique has been practiced, perfected and passed down among generations of traders.

6 Michael Phelps—*Beneath the Surface*: An Autobiography (with Brian Cazeneuve).Sports Publishing. New York. 2012.

7 Ryan Air, *First Quarter Financial Results*. 2013.

8 Maxwell, John. *Leadership Gold: Lessons I have learnt from a lifetime of leading*. Thomas Nelson Publishing. 2008.

9 Gaiman, Neil. *American Gods*. Headline Book Publishing. UK. 2001.

10 Bandler, Richard. *Get the Life You Want*. Harper Collins. UK. 2010.

11 Spark, Nick. *A History of Murphy's Law*. Lulu. 2006.

Chapter Four

1 Sagan, Carl. *Broca's Brain: Reflections on the Romance of Science.* Ballantine Books. 1980.

2 Amen, Daniel. *Change Your Brain, Change Your Body*. Harmony Books. USA. 2010.

3 Shaw, Bernard. *The Apple Cart—A Political Extravaganza*. Constable & Company. London 1930.

4 Singing Their Way to the White House: A Brief History of Campaign Songs. *TIME* Magazine. 2014. http://content.time.com. N.B. '*Don't Stop Thinking About Tomorrow*' was part of the Bill Clinton campaign song in 1992. The song was originally a Fleetwood Mac hit song in the USA during the 1970's.

5 McFadden, JohnJoe. The CEMI Field Theory: Closing the Loop. *Journal of Consciousness Studies*. 20(1). 2013. Pp 153-168.

6 Pockett, Susan. *The Nature of Consciousness: A Hypothesis*. Writers Club Press. 2000.

7 Bill Russell and Taylor branch. *Second Wind: The Memoirs of an Opinionated Man*. Random House. 1979.

8 Montapert, Alfred. *The Supreme Philosophy of Man: The Laws of Life*. Prentice Hall. 1970.

9 Siegel, Daniel. *The Developing Mind: How Relationships and the Brain Interact to Shape Who We Way Are*. The Guilford Press. 2012.

10 This technique is based just on personal experience and there is no guaranty about its effectiveness for everyone. If it is to be used at all by others, then it should be used with caution and only if individual health circumstances allow it.

11 Goleman, Daniel. *Emotional Intelligence: Why it Can Matter More Than IQ*. Bloomsbury Publishing Plc. 1996.

12 Google to buy Nest Labs for $3.2Billion. *Wall Street Journal*. Jan 13, 2014.

13 http://dominiqueansel.com/cronut-101.

14 The creative innovation remains in the creation of the cronut and not in the ensuing black market for the product. Intending customers are encouraged to make all purchases directly with the shop which owns the cronut patent.

Chapter Five

1 Patton, George, S. *War As I Knew It* (With an introduction by Rick Atkinson). Houghton Mifflin. New edition.1995.

2 Nevid, Jeffrey. *Psychology: Concepts and Applications*. Houghton Mifflin Company. USA. 2009. Pp478.

3 Pastorino, Ellen., Doyle-Portillo, Susann. *What is Psychology? Essentials*. Wadsworth. USA. 2013.Pp 472.

4 Hook, Derik. *Erickson's Psychosocial Stages of Development*. (In Watts, Jacki. Cockcroft, Kate and Duncan, Norman. Eds.) *Developmental Psychology*. UCT Press. South Africa. 2009.

5 Zastrow, Charles & Kirst-Ashman, Karen. *Understanding Human Behavior and the Social Environment*. Brooks/Cole. USA. 2010. Pp 121.

6 Davis, Stephen. & Buskist, William. (eds). *21st Century Psychology: A Reference Handbook*. Sage Publications. USA. 2008. Pp409.

7 Mondak, Jeffery. *Personality and the Foundations of Political Behavior.* Cambridge University Press. 2010. Pp24.

8 King, Daniel & Lawley, Scott. *Organizational Behaviour.* Oxford University Press. 2013. Pp 244.

9 In managing yourself, you do not have to be alone. The Junglepreneur Nation community is open to all Junglepreneurs who need companionship and support. Feel free to get in touch at any time through www.junglepreneur.com.

Chapter Six

1 '127 Hours: Director Danny Boyle Says You'd Cut Your Hand Off, Too' (Interview). *National Geographic Adventure.* Nov 4, 2010. http://adventureblog.nationalgeographic.com

2 Lakatos, Lyssie & Lakatos Shames, Tammy. *Fire Up Your Metabolism: 9 Proven Principles for Burning Fat and Losing Weight Forever.* Fireside. 2004. Pp135.

3 Miller, David. *Grow Youthful: Ancient Secrets, Modern Research.* D.N. Miller. 2003. Pp 202-203.

4 Long, A. *Epictetus: A Stoic and Socratic Guide to Life.* Oxford University Press. 2002.

5 'Whales Use Killer Technique for Hunting Fish'. *BBC News.* February 4, 2010. http://news.bbc.co.uk

6 Cooperative Dolphins Help Fishermen Catch Fish. *Discovery.* http://news.discovery.com. May 2, 2012

7 Roosevelt, Eleanor & Emblidge, David Blanche (Ed). With introduction by Blanche Wiesen Cook. *My Day: The Best of Eleanor Roosevelt's Acclaimed Newspaper Columns, 1936-1962.* Da Capo Press. 2001. Pp7.

8 Fiedler, Edgar. Across the Board: The Three R's of Economic Forecating—Irrational, irrelevant and Irreverent. *The Chartered Financial Analysts Digest.* 1977. 14(6).

9 Bloch, Authur. *Murphy's Law: The 26th Anniversary Edition:* Berkley Publishing Group. 2003.

10 Http://www.frogtek.org

Chapter Seven

1 Mehrabian, Albert. *Non Verbal communication.* Transaction Publishers. 1977.

2 Collett, Peter. *The Book of Tells: How to Read People's Minds from Their Actions.* Bantam Books. New York. 2003.

3 Theories of motivation include among others; McClelland's Acquired Needs Theory, Herzberg's Two Factor Theory, Maslow's Hierarchy of Needs Theory and Elton Mayo's Hawthorne Studies.

4 http://www.google.com/about/company/history

5 The John Lewin Story: Our Founder. *John Lewis.* http://www.johnlewispartnership.co.uk

6 Benedict, Ruth. *The Chrysanthemum and the Sword: Patterns of Japanese Culture.* Houghton Miffin Company. Boston 1946.

7 Kiyohide, Seki. The Circle of On, Giri and Ninjo: Sociologists Point of View. *The Annual Reports on Cultural Science.* Hokkaido University, Sapporo Japan. 1971. 19(2). Pp 105-108.

8 Nigeria—Globacom: Born to Rule the Telecom World. *Nokia Siemens Networks Newsletter.* https://www.siemens.be/cmc/newsletters

9 Gerber, Michael. *The E Myth Manager: Why Most Small Businesses Don't Work and What to Do About It.* Harper Collins. 2001.

10 Jantsch John. *Duct Tape Marketing.* Thomas Nelson. 2011.

11 Toyota. Just-in-Time—Philosophy of Complete Elimination of Waste. *The Toyota Corporation.* http://www.toyota-global.com

12 Bennet, Arnold. *How to Live 24 Hours a Day.* Arc Manor Publishing. USA. 2007(Reprint).

13 Stanhope, Philip Dormer. (Earl of Chesterfield). *The Works of Lord Chesterfield: Including His Letters to His Son.* Harper & Brothers. New York. 1838.

14 Man Eats Two Pounds of Metal a Day. *Weekly World News.* February, 11, 1997.

15 Kennedy, Robert, F. *Bobby Kennedy off Guard.* Grosset and Dunlap. 1968.

16 Renshaw, Jean. *Korean Women Managers and Corporate Culture: Challenging Tradition, Choosing Empowerment, Creating Change.* Routledge. New York. 2011. Pp 50.

17 http://www.sungjoogroup.com

18 Smith. N. *Managing Risk in Construction Projects.* Blackwell Sciences. Oxford. 1999.

19 Rumsfield, Donald. *Known and Unknown—A Memoir*. Sentinel/Penguin Group. 2011.

20 Adams, J. *Risk*. UCL Press, UK. 1995.

21 *Ibid.* note 1, chapter 1.

22 Coyle, B. *Risk Awareness and Corporate Governance*. IFS. 2002

23 Culp, C. *The Risk Management Process*. John Wiley. USA. 2001.

24 *Ibid.* note 1, chapter 1.

25 Crouhy, M. Galai, D. & Mark, R. *The Essentials of Risk Management*. McGraw Hill. USA. 2006

26 *Ibid.* note 1, chapter 1.

Chapter Eight.

1 Massai Warriors Take Meat From Lions. *Discovery*. http://www.discovery.com/tv-shows/human-planet.

2 Income into a region or country is not limited to this list of possible sources. It can include other sources which are specific to a location.

3 Aside from the government and large corporations, there can be other big spenders depending on the territory.

4 Skills are acquired abilities which you specifically chose, hone and practice over time for excellence. Talents are natural abilities which you are born with and in which you can excel through further practice or study. In addition to doing a personal skills audit you should also carry out a personal talent audit since this will enhance your overall personal development.

5 Angelou, Maya. Biographies and Poems: *Letter to My Daughter, Gather Together in My Name, I Shall Not Be Moved, Mom and Me and Mom, The Heart of a Woman, I know Why the Caged Bird Sings*. 2008, 2009, 2010, 2011, 2013.

6 The author is of the opinion that the conservation of wildlife, natural habitats and the environment is a priority for the entire human race. So the hunting referred to here implies authorised hunting of game only and not hunting just for the sake of it or for any illegal reasons.

7 Selfridge, Harry, Gordon. *Mr. Selfridge's Romance of Commerce:* (An Abridged Version of the Classic Text—Business and Life, 1918). Adams Media. 2013.

8 Geneen, Harold. *Managing*. Harper Collins Publishers.1986.

9 Soucek, Gayle. *Marshall Field's: The Store That Helped Build Chicago.* History Press, 2013.

10 Goddard, Leslie. *Images of America: Remembering Marshal Fields*. Arcadia Publishing. 2011.

Chapter Nine

1 Alpesh Patel—Working to Challenge Nokia, Blackberry and Samsung in Africa. *Forbes News*. 30, April, 2013. www.forbes.com

2 Japan—The Official Guide: Ukai—Comorant Fishing. *Japan National Tourism Organisation*. http://www.jnto.go.jp

3 Wasps v Moths: Biocontrol Uses Nature Against Crop Pests. *BBC News*. Jan 22, 2013. http://www.bbc.co.uk

4 Steve Jobs: The Five Apple Products that Changed the World. *The Telegraph*. Oct, 6, 2011. http://www.telegraph.co.uk

5 Overseas, iPhones are the Hot New Currency: Apple's Signature Product Has Become an International Currency. *Bloomberg News*. February 10, 2014.

6 Forbes Magazine. http://www.forbes.com

7 Einstein, Albert. *The World As I See It*. Covici Friede.1934. (Reprinted in 2011 by Open Road Media).

8 SEAL Code: A Warrior Creed. *US Navy Seals*. http://navyseals.com/nsw/seal-code-warrior-creed.

9 Beecher, Henry, W. *Lectures to Young Men on Various Important Subjects*. J.C Derby. New York. 1856.

10 Ford, Henry. *My Life and Work*. Angus and Robertson. 1923. (New Edition: Alan Kardec and Filiquarian Publishing. 2006).

11 Kelly, Fred. *The Wright Brothers—A Biography Authorised by Orville Wright*. Harcourt, Brace and Company. 1943. (Dover edition reproduced in1989.)

12 Kennelly, Arthur. Biographical Memoir of Thomas Alva Edison. *National Academy of Sciences*. 1932. pp. 300–301.

Chapter Ten

1 Riley, Pat. *The Winner Within—A Life Plan For Team Players.* Putnam's Sons. 1993.

2 Twain, Mark. *Autobiography of Mark Twain, Volume 1: The Complete and Authoritative Edition-Volume 10 of Mark Twain Papers.* (Smith, Harriet., Griffin, Benjamin., Fischer, Victor. & Frank, Michael. Eds.). University of California Press. 2010.

3 Mandela, Nelson. *Long Walk To Freedom - Volume 1.* Hachette. UK. 2009.

4 An interesting aspect of a visit to the Apartheid Museum in South Africa is the option to re-enact the apartheid period in South Africa from two sides of the then divide. i.e. The class of South Africans who had to live under the rules of Apartheid at that time and the class which did not. The tour offers a very subjective experience of what life was like for different people in South Africa then. It is also a fitting tribute to the huge sacrifice made by many for the South African Nation to achieve freedom.

5 Henley, William. *Poems by William Ernest Henley.* D. Nutt. 1919. (Reprinted by Kessinger Publishing in 2005).

6 Peale, Norman, Vincent. *The Power of Positive Thinking.* Cedar. UK. 1953.

7 Keller, Helen. *The Story of My Life.* New York Double Day, Page and Co. 1903. (Reprinted by Dover Publications in 1996).

8 Thomas, J. Watson Sr. – Biography. *IBM Corporation.* http://www-03.ibm.com/ibm/history/exhibits/chairmen/chairmen_3.html

9 *Ibid.* note 9, chapter 9.

10 The Presidents. *The White House, United States.* http://www.whitehouse.gov/about/presidents

11 Tate. Pablo Picasso: Artist Biography. *Tate Art Museum UK.* http://www.tate.org.uk/art/artists/pablo-picasso-1767

ACKNOWLEDGMENTS

It is said that it takes a whole town to get a good book ready, and this is so true. Therefore, this appreciation is to my own town of supportive people spread over the continents of Africa, Australasia, Europe, and North America. First, I am very grateful to the Omnipotent God, for the ability, talents, and opportunity given to me to put this book together. I'd also like to thank my darling wife, Ayodeji, and my wonderfully adventurous children, Edmund-David Adeite, Catherine Dahunsi and Elizabeth-Mary Idunnu. This is for being very supportive and patient with me all through the time-consuming and sometimes challenging period of writing the book. Adeite and Dahunsi would often come into my study many times to stay with me or offer to help me write the book. I would gratefully tell them to wait a few more years, but such joy helped me to pull through. My love and thanks also goes to my siblings and the extended Fasanya family represented by my brother Olusegun, for supporting me and this venture in one way or another. My dear mother, Caroline, has particularly been an immense pillar of support, and I say thank you so much, Mum, for always being there. I also cherish here the memory of my dear departed father, Samson Olusanya Fasanya (1931–2007). Dad, you helped sow the seeds for this book many years ago, by virtue of the all-around training you gave to me. Your essence lives on, and you are an ultimate Junglepreneur. I honor you.

To a valued role model, Paul Roberts, the author of *Guide to Project Management*, goes my sincere thanks for challenging me to dig deeper and stretch my concepts further during the initial manuscript development in

UK. Special gratitude goes to my dear friend, Nicholas Bakare, for his unrelenting encouragement, support and objective perspectives. I am also very grateful to another dear friend, Siji George, for constantly following up on me to ensure that I pace myself well, and take some time off from my crazy schedule when necessary. A great deal of appreciation also goes to Laurel Cohn and Siboney Duff (Sib), who did a fantastic job on editing the second draft of my manuscript all the way from Australia. Sib, your objective and professional comments helped my triangulation objectives for the book. I am also thankful to my web editor and brother, Kayode Fasanya (Chaka), for his techie work on the online representation of the book concepts and for transforming the vision from text into amazing graphics—great stuff. A great deal of appreciation also goes to Natasa Lekic, my editorial process manager, and to Dan Crissman, my overall book editor, who both worked with me from New York. Dan, accept my sincere gratitude for the excellent and selfless editing work you did on the final manuscripts.

I would also like to appreciate veteran publisher Randy Kuckuck for his wise and experienced guidance during the early production stages of this book. I am most grateful to Regan Parker, publishing services manager at Thomson-Shore, for coordinating all aspects of the book production. I am also grateful to Jerry Friends, the publishing services coordinator, for supervising critical stages in the book production. Special appreciation goes to the book production manager, Tod Baker, for his patient resilience in getting all aspects of the book production done to specification and time schedules. I would also like to specially thank Sheila Cowley, the graphic designer; Kiran Spees, the internal book designer; Trey Schorr, the title's copyeditor; and Ken and Jacinta Calcut, the book cover designers, for doing a fantastic job in their different areas. To my friend Barbara McNichol, expert editor and author of *Word Trippers*, I am truly appreciative of your efforts with the final polishing work done on aspects of the book profile. I would also like to congratulate Terrain Publishing UK on this first title published on a collaborative basis. Finally a great deal of thanks goes to so many other associates, in-laws, friends, role models, relatives, and supporters who are just too numerous to mention. I really appreciate each and every one of you for the great roles you played, and I am truly thankful.

Index

B

C

D

E

F

G

H

I

J

K

L

N

O

P

Q

R

S

T

U

V

W

www.ingramcontent.com/pod-product-compliance
Ingram Content Group UK Ltd.
Pitfield, Milton Keynes, MK11 3LW, UK
UKHW041830290726
14061UKWH00004BA/174/J